White Squaw

White Squaw

The True Story of Jennie Wiley

by Arville Wheeler

Illustrated by Ture Bengtz

Jesse Stuart Foundation
Ashland, Kentucky
2000

Library of Congress Cataloging-in-Publication Data

Wheeler, Arville, 1900–
   White Squaw : the true story of Jennie Wiley / by Arville Wheeler.
     p. cm.
   Summary: A fictionalized account of the life of Jennie Sellards Wiley, who spent a year as an Indian captive in Kentucky and eventually escaped and returned to her husband in Virginia.
   ISBN 0-945084-82-X
   1. Wiley, Jennie (Sellards) d. 1831--Juvenile fiction. [1. Wiley, Jennie (Sellards) d. 1831--Fiction. 2. Indians of North America--Captivities.] I. Title.

PZ7.W5585 Wh 2000
[Fic]--dc21   00-058739

Published By:
Jesse Stuart Foundation
P.O. Box 669 Ashland, KY 41105
(606) 326-1667

to L. V. W.

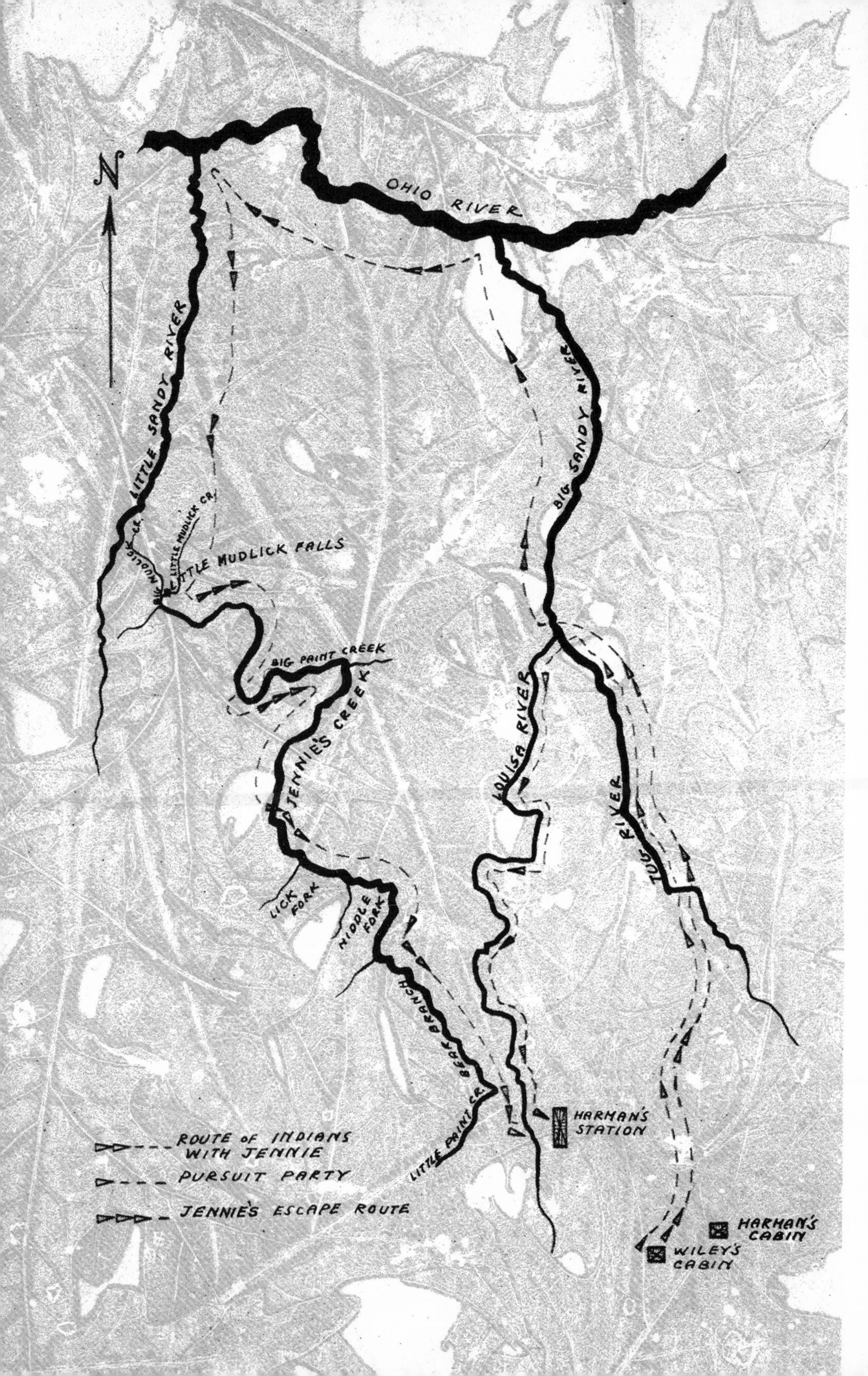

N

OHIO RIVER

LITTLE SANDY RIVER

BIG SANDY RIVER

MUDLICK

LITTLE MUDLICK CR.

LITTLE MUDLICK FALLS

BIG PAINT CREEK

JENNIE'S CREEK

LICK FORK

MIDDLE FORK

LITTLE PAINT CR.

BEAR BRANCH

LOUISA RIVER

TUG RIVER

HARMAN'S STATION

ROUTE OF INDIANS WITH JENNIE

PURSUIT PARTY

JENNIE'S ESCAPE ROUTE

HARMAN'S CABIN

WILEY'S CABIN

TABLE OF CONTENTS

Warnings   1

The Fight in the Forest   7

The Attack on the Cabin   14

The Chiefs' Quarrel   23

John Borders' Return   27

Plans for Rescue   32

Forced Marching for Jennie   38

The Second Night in Captivity   44

Indian Threats   50

Another Day of Marching   57

Tug River Crossing   63

The Rescue Party Outdistanced   67

Departure of the Cherokee   72

The Shawnee Chief as Medicine Man   78

On the March Again   82

At Little Mudlick Falls   87

Cooking for the Indians   91

The Bear Hunt   98

Trapping Small Game   103

Indian Visitors   108

Hundreds of Fish   112

Lead into Bullets   118

A Feast of Corn   122

Buffalo Robes and Deerskin Clothes   126

Return of the Cherokee   130

Torture   135

Five Hundred Silver Brooches   142

Jennie's Dream   146

A Break for Freedom   150

Moments of Suspense   154

Safe at Last   160

DEAR READERS

This book is not a product of the imagination. It is a story based on fact. All incidents in it have been authenticated. Those which could not be authenticated and about which there has been speculation have not been recorded. The omission of them adds to rather than detracts from the value of the story.

Names of all the principal characters are real. Families now living in the region in which this story has its setting still bear these names. The title, *White Squaw*, was, according to history, the name the Indians gave to Jennie Wiley from the moment they took her captive.

Many of the places described in the story remain today in their original state. The rockhouses at Cherokee and at Mudlick Falls are in the same condition as they were when White Squaw left them. Over the years weather conditions and the thoughtless scribbling of sightseers have removed Indian writings from their stony walls, but the rocks still stand. The tall poplar, spruce, sycamore, and beech trees that once lifted their leafy boughs above Mudlick Falls are gone, no doubt, but trees like them stand where they stood. Yes, the story is true.

Just imagine that you were living almost 200 years ago. Can you? Then, as you read this story and turn page after page, you will see how the dauntless courage of a pioneer woman, with tremendous odds against her, finally triumphed over the Indians. You will see real Indian fighting taking place before your very eyes the very minute you read about it.

I believe you will get the thrill out of the story that I got when my Grandmother Wheeler first told it to me.

Sincerely yours,

Arville Wheeler

4428 Lealand Lane
Nashville, Tennessee

*"Jennie! Jennie!" a voice called
outside the cabin. It was a man's voice.*

WARNINGS

Jennie! Jennie!" a voice called outside the cabin. It was a man's voice, low, as if the speaker were half afraid of being overheard. And yet who, unless he were within a few paces, could have heard any sound above the wind which whistled around the corners of the cabin and through the open space between the cabin's two rooms?

Inside the cabin Jennie Wiley heard it and stopped weaving. She placed the threaded shuttle upon the new cloth in front of her. All day long she had been weaving the linsey-woolsey material which was to be used for winter clothes. A few minutes more and the length of material would have been finished.

Three small children dropped pieces of kindling with which they had been building make-believe cabins and looked toward their mother. The fourth, a baby of fifteen months, crawled across the room to her. He pulled at the hem of her long skirt and looked at her pleadingly. His little lips were puckered but no sound escaped them although

1

his eyes plainly said, "Pick me up, Mama! Pick me up!"

"It's all right, Tommy," Jennie assured him. "That is Uncle John Borders at the door. You know Uncle John." What, she wondered, could bring John here in this awful downpour of rain!

Jennie pushed the short, split-log bench away from the loom. She took the child in her arms. "We'll open the door for Uncle John," she said, patting the child's back gently with her right hand.

"Let me open the door," said Batt Sellards, laying aside the piece of split-hickory he had been shaping into an ax handle.

Batt was Jennie's youngest brother. He was fifteen years old and as brave a lad as ever lived in the Virginia backwoods. He was tall, straight, slender, and handsome. Batt was not his real name, but a nickname. He had first been called Batt by Jennie's little daughter Ruth, who couldn't say his real name. The nickname stuck, and he became known as Batt Sellards by every settler in Walker's Gap.

From the brackets on either side of the door, Batt lifted the hickory crossbar and leaned it against the wall. Then he turned the big wooden buttons at top and bottom and pulled the heavy door open. It creaked on its wooden hinges as it swung inward.

"John Borders, you are wet to the skin!" said Batt. "What brings you here in this terrible weather?"

The water ran down John's leather jacket and dropped off its fringed edges. His coonskin cap was soaking wet. It looked more like the racoon itself than like a cap.

"Come in," said Jennie, who was still holding Tommy in her arms. "Come in, John, and warm yourself."

John Borders shook himself, and drops of water, like the first big drops in a summer shower, fell on the floor about him. "It's a wet day," he said, as he walked to the huge

2

fireplace, where blazing logs threw out warmth and comfort. He turned his back to the fire. His long arms hung loosely at his side. He rubbed the fringed edges of his hunting jacket between the tips of his long, bony fingers. In the heat of the open fire, dampness steamed from his clothes like mist.

"What's on your mind, John?" Batt asked.

"Yes," said Jennie. "What brings you here on a day like this?"

"Indians, Jennie!" answered John Borders, "I fear the Indians are about."

"What makes you think so?" asked Jennie. "Tell us about it."

So John told them how, that morning, he had left his cabin at the break of day. He had gone into the forest in search of sheep that had escaped from the fold the night before. Following their trail had been easy for a time. They had left footprints. Here and there they had pawed leaves to get at the tasty leaf of the teaberry plant. Bits of wool had been left hanging to the thorns of the wild crab apple and the hawthorn bushes. But toward noon, rain had begun to fall. It was a slow drizzle at first. Then it came down harder — the chilly rain of November. It washed away signs of hoofprints. It hung like drops of crystal to twigs and to bits of wool alike, making it hard to tell one from the other. Low-hanging clouds covered the hilltops. Pockets of fog formed in the narrow valleys and in the deep hollows. One could see hardly any distance at all.

But sheep were the pioneers' most valuable possession. They furnished wool for clothing and, when other food was scarce, meat for the table. Wolves had made so many raids on the flocks at Walker's Gap that neither John Borders nor the other settlers could afford to lose any more sheep, if they could help it. So John had kept up the search.

3

Toward midafternoon he had stopped under an oak tree, trying to think where to look next. Suddenly, through the rain, he had heard the hooting of owls on the ridges nearby. The hootings came first from one ridge and then from another. They were rhythmically spaced. They seemed like signals.

Signals! The thought had startled him. Signals! Of course they were signals! Signals of the Shawnee Indians!

The Shawnees, he knew, used many signals of this kind — the call of birds and the cry of wild beasts. They had a signal for every occasion, a signal suitable to the event and to the weather. Suitable to the weather! Owls often hoot on rainy days. The more he had thought about it, and listened, the surer he had become that the hootings were Shawnee signals.

4

In that case the settlement must be in danger of attack by the Indians. The settlers must be warned. There was no time to lose, for the Indians must already be close at hand — close enough for him to hear their signals — and the settlement was almost defenseless. Thomas Wiley, Jennie's husband, had gone to the trading post.

The Harmans — Tice, Daniel, George, and Henry — were all away on the short hunt, the hunt of two or three weeks that the hunters always made in order to lay in meat for their families for the winter. Even the Harmans' father, Henry Harman himself, was away on the short hunt. So were Henry Skaggs, James Skaggs, Sid Damron, and Allen Draper. Was there another man in the settlement? He tried to think. But that, he had realized, was beside the point. The settlers must be warned; first Jennie and her children — they were nearest — and then the others.

Jennie listened quietly while her brother-in-law told his story. She had lived close to danger all her life. She knew how to face it. Her father had moved his family from the Shenandoah Valley to Walker's Gap when Jennie was only three years old, but she remembered well an attack of the Indians at that time. Her mother had poked her into the hollow of a beech tree, where she had remained without making a sound until the skirmish was over.

Many times, before she was grown up, there had been attacks upon the settlement and upon the family. Once an Indian had tried to seize her as she returned from the spring

5

with a bucket of water, but she had dashed the water in his face and escaped. On more than one occasion since her marriage, she had defended her own brood. Yes, Jennie Wiley knew the Indians and had good reason to fear them.

She brushed her hair back from her forehead. "What would you suggest we do, John?" she asked.

"I think you had better go to our house for the night, Jennie," John answered. "I'm afraid the Indians plan an attack upon the settlement before morning. We will be in a better position to defend ourselves if we all stay together. I believe the Indians have already had a skirmish with the hunters and have been forced to flee in many directions in order to throw the hunters off their trail. The signals must mean that they are now getting back together at a spot agreed upon. They may strike at any time."

"I expect Thomas back before very late tonight," said Jennie. "He left for the trading post before daylight this morning. It would be dreadful for him to find no one here on his return. We must wait for him here. Then we can all come together. Besides, John, the Indians never attack in daylight."

"I tell you, Jennie, you won't be safe here," said John. "You can't be sure what the Indians will do. Maybe they won't attack — maybe they will. As for Thomas, we can stop him as he passes our house on the way home. It will save him two miles each way. Not far to be sure, except for a tired man at the end of a long day."

"Are you sure you can see Thomas from your house and stop him?" asked Jennie.

"Of course," John answered. "He passes close by the house."

"Very well, then," said Jennie. "Batt and I will do the chores and then we will come. You must not wait for us. You must warn the others."

6

THE FIGHT IN THE FOREST

John Borders had been right in his guess about a skirmish between the Indians and the men from the settlement.

On reaching the hunting grounds where they planned to stay for several weeks, the hunters had set up a temporary shelter. This they needed as protection from the weather, from prowling animals, and also from Indians.

The camp was built of heavy poles, notched and fitted together. It was ten by fourteen feet in size and about ten feet high. An open space in one side was used for a door. The roof over the top was made of poles, boughs, and branches.

The camp was located in a narrow bottom near a stream which skirted a high hill. From inside the camp, through small openings in the walls, the men had a view for some distance on all four sides. This made it difficult for an enemy to take them unawares.

7

Their first night in camp was rainy, and morning dawned cold and wet and cloudy. Some of the men decided to hunt in spite of the weather, while the others stayed behind to set their gear in place, to store the furs and hides which they had collected on the way, and to make the camp as weatherproof as possible.

The four Harman brothers — Daniel, George, Matthias, and young Henry — were among those who went out to hunt. Though all the Harmans were expert hunters, Matthias, or "Tice" as he was called by his companions, was the most expert.

Tice had thick yellow hair, cold blue eyes set in a thin, sharp face, and a large nose. Though small in stature, he was bold and fearless, and able to endure any kind of weather or hardship. Early in life he had become a hunter and had ranged the woods far and near. He had taken a leading part in all the expeditions of the settlers, whether for hunting, for exploration, or for warfare. He was a dead shot with his rifle, and through many encounters with the Indians he had become as crafty as they. He could outguess and outwit them as no one else in the company could. Tice was the unquestioned leader of the hunting party. Nothing could have kept him in camp that morning.

Probably nothing could have kept old Henry Harman in camp, either, except that he knew, better than anyone, what still needed to be done there. For old Henry was a great hunter, too. If Tice had learned many things from his own experience, much of his skill in hunting and in woodcraft was due to his father's teaching. No one had been a greater hunter and woodsman than old Henry Harman in his youth.

Henry had brought his dog, Savage, with him on this hunting trip. Savage had been trained in tracking Indians, and he could be counted on to give warning of their approach long before they could be seen.

8

While those who had stayed behind were busying them-selves about the camp, Savage became uneasy. He sniffed the air. He whined. The hair on his back stood on end.

"What is it, Savage?" asked Henry. "Indians?"

The dog continued to whine and to bristle. He looked anxiously toward the hill on the other side of the stream, ran to Henry with short, sharp barks, then turned again, growling, to face the hill. A party of Indians were just coming over the top.

The men went into the camp and prepared to defend themselves. They took up their positions and thrust their long rifles through some of the small openings which had been left in the walls for that very purpose.

Peering over the sights of his long rifle, old Henry was the first to see an Indian slipping through the bushes near the camp. A shot from his rifle found its mark. The Indian bounded into the air, fell forward on his face, and never moved again.

At just about that time, Tice Harman was standing be-hind the butt end of an uprooted tree not very far from the camp. He held a deer's antler in each hand. He rubbed the antlers over each other, scraped one upon the other, and knocked them together.

The noise he made was like the clashing of antlers when two bucks are engaged in a life-and-death struggle. "If there is a deer within hearing distance," Tice said to him-self, "it will soon be heading this way."

He laid the antlers down upon the ground and picked up his rifle. He stood motionless behind the uprooted tree. He did not move so much as a finger, for nothing turns a deer from its course more quickly than a rustle or movement of any kind.

Presently Tice saw, through the alder bushes, a buck with great, spreading antlers. It ran swiftly but silently. When

9

it was within twenty paces of Tice, it stopped and turned its head in his direction. It looked at Tice with its big dark eyes but seemed not to see him. Its left hind foot was uplifted. No hunter could have asked for a more certain target.

Quietly Tice cocked his flintlock and aimed it at a white spot just behind the deer's left foreleg. Just then there was the sound of a rifle shot in the direction of the hunter's camp. Tice did not pull the trigger. Instead he eased the hammer down upon the powder and lowered his rifle.

One of the rules on hunts of this kind was that men left at camp were to use their firearms only when there was need to call the hunters back to camp. A shot from that direction, then, could mean only one thing: the presence of Indians.

Tice climbed upon the log behind which he had been hiding. He took his hunter's horn from his belt and held it to his lips. He blew a loud trumpet-like blast that sounded and resounded through the forest.

From the thickets in various directions came the other hunters. They, too, had heard the rifle shot and knew its meaning.

"It's the pesky Indians," Tice said to them when they were assembled. "Probably it's the ornery Cherokee chief with his band on his way to the Tennessee villages; the one who is always stealing our horses and cattle when he passes the settlement."

"Our women and children, too," Henry Skaggs added. "Remember how Mrs. Tacket was dragged from her bed in the middle of the night and never heard of again."

"That's right!" said George Harman. "We've got to stop them now or we'll never know what's going to happen."

Tice pushed back his coonskin cap and pulled at his nose thoughtfully. "We'll have to get back to camp as warily as we can and as fast as we can," he said. "If we surround them before they know we're there, maybe we can stop them today. I believe we can if the men at the camp can hold them off until we get there."

Tice Harman and his men scattered themselves in the forest about the camp and crept up on the enemy so warily that no rustling leaf or breaking twig gave warning of their approach. They took positions behind trees where they were able to fire from many directions.

The Indians, although outnumbering the hunters three to one, were at a disadvantage. They were between the men in the camp and the men in the forest. If they dodged behind trees to escape bullets from one direction, they became targets for bullets from another direction.

This situation was just what Tice Harman had hoped for. Now he had the Indians where he wanted them. Their only means of escape lay in a bold dash for the hills, and even then the hunters could follow them and might do great damage.

Patiently Tice and his men waited. Each time an Indian exposed himself to view, he was shot down by one of the hunters.

At last the Cherokee chief had to change his tactics. He gave his warriors orders to cease shooting into the camp that protected Henry Harman and his men and to fight the hunters who, in positions behind trees and clumps of bushes, now had them completely surrounded.

George Harman was the first of the hunters to engage in a hand-to-hand fight with an Indian. While he was in a crouched position trying to reload his rifle, a warrior slipped up behind him with lifted tomahawk. George, seeing his danger just in time, lunged at his enemy and seized him by the ankles. The two of them rolled over and over, first one on top and then the other. They were equally matched in strength, and each of them knew that this was a life-and-death struggle.

At one moment, when George seemed to be getting the worst of it, someone cried, "Turn him loose, George, and flee for your life!"

"When you see me whipped by an Indian, it will be time for all of us to flee," cried George. With a desperate effort, he freed one hand from the Indian's grasp and put an end to his enemy with his hunting knife.

In the meantime Henry Harman had come outside the camp and was fighting in the open. The Cherokee chief saw him and recognized him as the father of Tice Harman. "Old Henry," he shouted. "Ugh!" Then he shot four arrows in Henry's direction so fast that the fourth arrow was in the air before the first one had struck the old man in the chest. One after another the arrows penetrated the heavy leather jacket and pierced the old man's chest. Old Henry was so badly wounded that he could not stand without leaning against a tree, but he continued shooting his rifle while his son George, who had managed to reach his side, kept reloading it for him.

Meanwhile young Henry Harman, ramming a bullet down the muzzle of his rifle, was seen by the son of the Cherokee chief. The young prince aimed an arrow at close range, but before he could release the bowstring, he was killed by a bullet from the rifle of Tice Harman.

The Cherokee chief saw his son fall. With a wild cry of grief, he raised the slender, lifeless body of the young Indian in his arms. Holding him there, he shouted out orders to his band of followers. Part of them must take the body of the young prince to his home north of the Ohio for burial. The others must follow him to the settlement, where they would wreak vengeance on the family of Harman; such vengeance, indeed, as had never been dreamed of.

At these words the Cherokee turned and, followed by the others, fled toward the hills. The fight was over.

Tice Harman sent a small party of hunters in pursuit of the fleeing Indians, while he himself stayed behind to do what he could for his father, who was now in great pain. A short time later the hunters returned. "The Indians have fled in so many directions that it is impossible to follow their trail," they reported.

"That is an old Indian trick," Tice answered. "They will come together later at some point agreed upon." He thought a moment, then added, "I know as well as the Cherokee does where he is going. We must break camp at once and return to the settlement."

Hurriedly he gave orders to make a litter for his father.

Quickly the litter was made and the old man was placed upon it. Choosing two strong men to bear it, Tice said to them, "Carry him to his home in Ab's Valley. The rest of us will get to the settlement as fast as we can."

Old Henry Harman looked at his son. "I'm all right, son," he said. "You go after the Indians. Track 'em down. Get 'em all, every last one of 'em."

As soon as the furs and hides could be tied in bundles and placed upon pack horses, Tice Harman and his hunters headed for Walker's Gap.

THE ATTACK ON THE CABIN

Soon we will be ready to go, Tommy," Jennie said to her baby. She put a hooded cape around his tiny shoulders and tied the strings under his chin. "We'll be off for Uncle John's house in no time now." She patted Tommy on the back and kissed him. "You're a good boy," she said. "The best boy in the world."

Jennie idolized her four children, Hezekiah, Ruth, Naomi, and Thomas. Hezekiah was named for his grandfather, Hezekiah Sellards; Ruth and Naomi each had a name from the Bible; and Thomas was named for his father.

While she was getting Tommy ready, Hezekiah and Ruth had dressed themselves snugly in their heavy coats of home-spun linsey-woolsey and put on their stocking caps and yarn mittens. Naomi, whom Batt had helped into her out-of-doors garments, stood beside them. Batt himself was dressed in his leather hunting jacket with leggings to match. A hunting knife was thrust in his belt. A coonskin cap was pulled down over his ears.

14

After John Borders had left the cabin, Batt had banked the fire for the night. First he had rolled two huge logs, a backlog and a fore log, into place. Then he had piled pieces of burning wood in between these two logs and covered them with ashes. The fire would smolder until morning when, if all went well, Jennie and her family would return.

Jennie threw her heavy cape about her shoulders and tied the strings under her chin. She put on a fur bonnet which she had made with her own hands. In fact, she had made all of the clothing for the family except the shoes they wore. Those were made by her husband.

Everybody was ready now — ready and happy. It was a family custom to visit relatives on a Saturday night, and the children always looked forward to these visits. But a visit in the middle of the week was an unexpected occasion for them, and they were eager and excited. There was still plenty of time to reach Uncle John's house before dark. And as Indians had seldom, if ever, been known to attack in broad daylight, Jennie did not even think of worrying about them.

Batt reached for the hickory pole with which the door was barred. Then he drew back without touching it. Jennie's dog sniffed at the crack under the door and growled.

"What is it, Batt?" asked Jennie.

Before Batt could answer there was a war whoop outside the door — the war whoop of Indians!

"Merciful goodness!" Jennie started to shout, but she checked the words and said under her breath, "Indians."

Jennie had learned to control her emotions in the face of attack by the Indians. She knew that to have life she must be ready to fight for it. She knew that she must keep calm and unafraid.

"Let's pile everything in the house against the door," said Jennie. "We must keep them out as long as possible."

15

"Yes, we must," Batt answered.

On the side of the room opposite the door stood the heavy oak dining table. Together, Batt and Jennie carried it across the room and set it against the door. Then they carried over the split-log benches, on which the family sat at mealtime, and the wooden stools, and piled them on the table.

"What next?" asked Batt. Then, answering his own question, he added, "The firewood."

One corner of the room had been stacked full of firewood. Great logs five or six feet long had been piled to a height of about four feet. One at a time these logs were stacked under the table against the door. Then every other loose thing in the room was piled against the barricade.

"This should keep them out for a while," said Batt.

"It should," Jennie answered.

It was steadily growing darker and now, inside the cabin, Jennie and Batt could barely see each other.

Outside the cabin the yelling and whooping kept up. Neither Batt nor Jennie could see what was going on, for the cabin had been well chinked, but they knew what the Indians were doing. They were going through the war dance. That, as Jennie well knew, meant death for them all if, in spite of the barricade, the Indians managed to enter the cabin. How could she prevent it? Her mind went back to the earliest time she could ever remember, the time when she used to kneel beside her father at bedtime and say after him a prayer for God's care during the night. She had been taught to pray on other occasions, too, and she had taught her children to pray after her, "Not my will, but Thine be done." She bowed her head and repeated these words to herself.

There was a lunge against the door, scarcely noticeable inside the room. There were other lunges, soon followed

16

by the pounding of tomahawks. Then came the sound of chopping.

There was nothing that Batt and Jennie could do but watch and wait and pray. They had no firearms with which to defend themselves. Thomas Wiley's rifle lay on the gun rack above the fireplace, but it was not loaded, and there was neither powder nor lead in the cabin. Thomas had used the last of it the night before when he had shot a wolf that was prowling around his sheepfold. That morning he had left before break of day for the trading post, where he would exchange the herbs and ginseng root that he and Jennie had dug in the forest for powder, lead, salt, and other supplies needed for the winter ahead.

Batt picked up the piece of hickory which he had been shaping into an ax handle, and Jennie seized a three-legged stool. With these as their only weapons they waited and listened with little real hope that their barricade would keep the Indians out for long.

Crash! Crash! Crash! Blows fell upon the heavy door of the cabin — blows that shook the cabin from sill to rafter. Black walnuts came dropping through cracks in the loft, where they had been stored for winter use. Plop! Plop! Plop! They hit upon the wide, rough-hewn floor boards. Rings of dried pumpkin, hung on sticks that had been driven between the logs above the fireplace, slipped off the sticks and dropped on the hearth.

"What are the Indians battering the door with?" asked Jennie.

"I think it's the tree trunk I cut the backlog from," said Batt. "If it is, they'll knock the door off its hinges in no time."

Crash! Crash! Crash! The blows continued to fall upon the door.

Jennie bowed her head. "Dear God," she said, "if it be Thy will, spare us from the Indians; nevertheless, not my will but Thine be done."

Her prayer gave her strength and courage.

The pounding continued. It was too dark for Batt or Jennie to see the wooden pegs in the door's wooden hinges, but they knew they would soon be loosened. There was a tremendous crash and the sound of splitting timbers. The battering-ram came crashing through the heavy door. Firewood, table, and split-log benches were flung to the four sides of the room.

In came the Indians, the Cherokee chief in the lead. Enraged by the death of his son, the Cherokee had determined to seek revenge by wiping out the family of his enemy, Tice Harman. On reaching the settlement after the fight in the forest, he and his band had mistaken the Wileys' cabin for that of the Harmans. Once they had gained entrance they were in no mood to spare the life of anyone.

18

It was not long before Jennie and Tommy, whom she held in her arms, were the only ones left alive.

Jennie held her baby under her left arm while she defended herself with her right, wielding the three-legged stool in great arcs. One bronzed warrior after another fell to the floor under the impact of her blows. But still the fighting went on. A flying tomahawk thrown from the further side of the room narrowly missed her. She ducked another, hearing its thud as it buried itself in the wall behind her.

At that moment the Cherokee chief stepped forward, his tomahawk in his uplifted right hand. In his left was a rifle with which he warded off Jennie's blows. Back and forth they sparred, the fighting mother and the angry savage. The others, stunned by Jennie's ferocious fighting, fell back and watched in amazement. Could it be that the squaw of the white man was a match for their war chief?

The battle continued. Jennie fought to save the life of her baby. The Cherokee chief fought to avenge the death of his son. Neither one nor the other could think of anything else.

A Delaware warrior, feeling warmth from the fireplace, realized that the fire was not dead. He kicked the forestick back and forth with his right foot. The banked ashes trickled down between the logs and a bright flame shot up and burned with a steady glow. It shone upon Jennie's face.

Jennie was tall and slender. Her bonnet had fallen back in the struggle and revealed her long black hair, parted in the middle and done in a knot at the back of her head. The light from the fire gave it a reddish glow. Her eyes were black, her cheekbones high, her nose prominent. Was it true,

as some people said, that her mother was half Cherokee? She was strangely beautiful.

Whether it was her likeness to an Indian woman or something else that attracted attention, Jennie never knew. But suddenly an Indian — an old chief whom she had scarcely noticed up to this time — stepped between her and the Cherokee chief. With his right arm thrust out against the Cherokee, he knocked the stool from Jennie's hand with his left and, seizing her wrist, held her hand high and spoke words which stopped the battling at once.

THE CHIEFS' QUARREL

The two chiefs faced each other.

The Cherokee, six feet tall in his beaded moccasins, was big and powerful, with broad shoulders and hard, cruel features. He was, perhaps, fifty years of age. Around his head, a band of bright-colored cloth held a crown of feathers in place, and in his ears were silver rings of elaborate workmanship. He wore a red shirt and buckskin leggings. A hunting knife was stuck in his belt and he still held his tomahawk in his right hand. Though he preferred bow and arrows, he carried a white man's rifle, with shot pouch and powder horn slung over his left shoulder.

The other chief, who, by his gesture, had claimed Jennie as his captive, was less than six feet tall. He was an old man but, as was evident from his bold defiance of the Cherokee, he was still strong and fearless. He, too, wore the silver

23

rings and brooches of a chief as well as the ornaments of a medicine man and Indian priest. By the design on his beaded moccasins, Jennie knew him to be a Shawnee. Though bold and stern in his defiance, Jennie sensed in him a kindliness quite different from the savage fierceness of the Cherokee. She had known from the moment she had set eyes upon him that she could expect no mercy from the Cherokee, but she felt no fear of the Shawnee chief. He had come between her and certain death and, although he still held her wrist in a vise-like grip, he made no move to harm her. She felt that she could trust him and she made no further effort to resist.

The Cherokee chief was the first to break the tense silence that followed the Shawnee's challenge. His voice was angry and menacing. The Shawnee answered in a quiet voice, but it was plain to Jennie that he had little success in lessening the fury of the Cherokee. Though she did not understand their words, she was sure that the life of herself and her baby depended on the outcome of the argument.

The other Indians began to take places beside the two chiefs. Jennie watched them and sensed that they were taking sides according to their loyalties. She looked at the different designs on their moccasins and realized, for the first time, that four tribes were represented. There were two Cherokees, three Shawnees, three Delawares, and three Wyandottes in the mongrel band. The Delawares and the Cherokee sided with the Cherokee chief. The Shawnees and the Wyandottes stood beside the Shawnee chief. It looked as if Indian were about to fight Indian.

As the argument continued, the Cherokee chief became more and more infuriated. Through his angry shouting came, again and again, the name of Harman. Suddenly Jennie realized that the Indians had planned an attack, not on the Wiley family but on the home of Tice Harman.

24

Though the two chiefs had been speaking in the Indian language, Jennie thought that both the Cherokee and the Shawnee might speak and understand some English. It was worth trying, anyway, so she said, "This is not the home of Tice Harman!"

For a moment the argument ceased, and Jennie hoped that her words might win freedom for her. However, they seemed to have the opposite effect on the Cherokee chief, who shouted in still greater fury, stamping his feet and shaking his fist. As the Cherokee's rage increased, the Shawnee chief became firmer in his reply and more determined in his manner.

The next few moments were tense moments for all. The other Indians stood by, each ready to do the bidding of his chosen leader. As the argument went on, it finally became clear to Jennie that the Cherokee was willing to take the white squaw along as a captive, but insisted upon the death of the papoose.

Jennie turned to the Shawnee chief. "Don't let him kill my baby," she pleaded.

"Indians go fast," said the Shawnee chief. "Papoose die."

"Oh, please! Please! Save my baby!" Jennie pleaded. "I'll carry papoose and keep up. I promise."

Again the Shawnee chief turned to the Cherokee with words of explanation, and again an argument followed, this time less violent than before. At last the Cherokee chief gave in to the wishes of the Shawnee. He turned to his warriors with final directions.

At his words the Indians began to pile things in the middle of the floor. They slit the feather bed and the pillows with their tomahawks until feathers flew about the room like snowflakes. They dragged the burning logs from the fireplace and set the pile on fire. As it began to burn, they threw onto it everything they could lay their hands on.

25

They yelled and shouted with satisfaction. For though they had failed in their plan to attack the family of Tice Harman, they had wreaked vengeance upon the Walker's Gap settlement. They had killed four members of one family and destroyed their home. Two other members they were carrying off into captivity.

As they set out upon the long journey which was to take them north of the Ohio River, the Cherokee chief headed the line of march. Behind him in single file walked the nine warriors. Jennie, clasping her child in her arms, was the eleventh person in line. The old Shawnee chief walked behind her. In this order the procession started up the steep mountainside behind the Wiley cabin.

JOHN BORDERS' RETURN

After getting Jennie's promise to bring her family to his cabin as soon as the chores were done, John Borders set out for home. He took time on the way to warn as many of the neighbors as he could, but he knew he must get home as soon as possible in case the Indians were planning an attack on his own family. It was well after dark when he finally reached his cabin. He gave the usual knock on the door — three raps with a short pause between them, followed by two quick raps.

His wife Delilah lifted the heavy pole from its accustomed place across the door and turned the large wooden buttons that held it at the top and bottom. As she pulled the door open, John entered quickly and looked around the room.

"Where is Jennie?" he asked anxiously.

"Jennie!" said Delilah. "I haven't seen her. Did you expect to find her here?"

"Yes, I did," John replied. He started to say something else, but hesitated. Then he added, "I told her to get here before dark. It has been dark now for some time."

"Is something wrong, John?" asked Delilah. "What is it? Has anything happened to Jennie?"

"I don't know," he answered. "I hope not."

He walked back and forth across the narrow room, running his fingers through his hair nervously. It was clear that he was worried and upset.

"John," said Delilah. "What is the trouble?"

"Indians," he answered.

"Indians?" Delilah gasped.

"I am afraid so," said John. "I'm afraid Jennie may have been attacked by the Shawnee Indians. The hills were full of them this afternoon. They were signaling to one another all along the ridges. They seemed to be signaling from every peak and hilltop."

"What signal were they using?" Delilah asked.

"They were hooting like owls," said John.

"Owls!" exclaimed Delilah. "You must be right, John. That's the signal they would most likely use on a day like this."

"I warned Jennie," said John. "She and Batt were alone with the children. I made her promise to be here before dark. That was two hours ago."

"You must go back and see about them," said Delilah. "But not alone. You must take someone with you."

"There's not another man in the settlement," John replied. "They are all on the hunt with Tice Harman — all except Thomas Wiley, and he is at the trading post."

"What about Richard Skaggs?" Delilah questioned. "He's almost a man."

"That's right!" her husband replied. "And Richard will be glad to go with me. But you, Delilah. How can I leave you?"

Delilah looked at him and said quietly, "Don't worry, John. I'm sure the Indians won't come here, especially on a

28

night like this. It is too far from their usual path. Besides, with Jennie and Batt and the four children there are six lives to consider, you know."

"Yes," said John. "Yes, I must go. Keep the door barred, Delilah, and shield the lights from the windows. I'll be back as soon as I can — with good news, I hope."

John pulled his water-soaked cap over his head and ears and opened the door. Once outside he waited to hear the bar set in place. Then he was on his way to the Skaggs' cabin.

When he arrived, he found Richard Skaggs seated on a bench at the table with his mother and the younger children. He was eating bread and milk, which he dipped from a wooden bowl with a wooden spoon. He was fifteen years old, tall and awkward, but as fine a boy as there was in the settlement.

"Richard!" John Borders called outside the cabin.

"Yes, John," the young man answered, recognizing John Borders' voice and stepping to the door. In a moment he had unbarred it, and John Borders was inside the cabin.

Miranda Skaggs, Richard's mother, listened while John related the incidents of the afternoon. Her children were still seated at the table, their half-filled bowls of bread and milk set before them. As John Borders talked, they held their wooden spoons in their hands, their supper forgotten.

"Richard, you must go with John," Miranda said to her son when John Borders had finished his story. "You must go with him and see about Jennie and the children. We'll be all right. We have nearer neighbors than Jennie, and the Indians never come so close to the settlement as this."

"Yes, Mother," the youth replied.

Richard drew on his leather leggings and his hunting jacket. He thrust his hunting knife in his belt and picked up his rifle. "All ready, John," he said.

The night was black. Rain continued to fall, blown into great sheets by the wind. But darkness and rain did not matter to John Borders and Richard Skaggs, for they knew every path in the settlement. They followed the trail that led to the Wiley cabin until they reached the top of the hill. There they stopped to listen. There was no sound except that of the falling rain.

Cautiously, as if each step might bring them within striking distance of the enemy, they started down the path on the other side of the hill. As they drew near the cabin, Richard whispered to his companion, "I can smell something burning."

"So can I," John Borders answered. "It smells like burning cloth."

Richard pulled his hunting knife from its sheath and held it in his right hand. "Let's be ready, John," he whispered.

"Yes, Richard," John answered.

In a matter of minutes, though the time seemed longer to them, they came to the clearing where the Wiley's cabin stood. A faint light was shining through the doorway, but there was no sound or sign of life.

"The Indians have been here," John said. "We may be too late."

At these words Richard tightened his grip on the handle of his hunting knife, and the two of them crept toward the half-burned cabin where, a few hours earlier, John had stood before the barred door calling, "Jennie! Jennie!"

Now, when they reached it, they found the door broken down; the wall around it, shattered. Inside the cabin a fire was still smoldering in the middle of the room. It had burned the floor away under it, and flames had licked at the loft above until the loft had fallen in. A hole burned in the roof had let rain into the cabin, but the fire had been burning so fiercely that even the heavy rain could not com-

30

pletely put it out. By the flicker of an occasional flame John and Richard could see that the home of Jennie Wiley was an empty shell. Stools, benches, tables — all the Wileys' possessions — lay in ruins on that smoldering pile in the middle of the room.

"Well," said John Borders, finally breaking the dreadful silence that had fallen on them, "we'll have to find out!"

Richard knew what he meant. The words voiced his own thoughts, and the two men entered the cabin. They stepped carefully, searching, searching by the feeble light of the dying fire. And they found the bodies of the four who had been killed.

"Where are the others?" asked Richard.

"They must be here," John whispered. "They must be here. Not one of them could have been left alive."

For a moment John and Richard stood without speaking. Not a sound broke the silence except the drumming of rain on the roof and the steady drip, drip of water both inside and outside the cabin.

They continued their search. At last John whispered, "No, it's no use. They must have been taken by the Indians. In that case, there is nothing more that we can do here until daylight comes. But all the other settlers must be warned. The Indians may still be in the neighborhood. They may even be planning other attacks. I must get home as soon as I can to waylay Thomas Wiley and keep him from going further. You let your friends know what has happened and get them to carry the warning."

"Yes," agreed Richard. "I will."

And so, within the hour, fast runners — young friends of Richard Skaggs — were on their way to every cabin in the settlement. By daylight every household for miles around knew of the fate of Jennie Wiley and of the danger of further attack by the Indians.

31

PLANS FOR RESCUE

Home once again, John Borders hung a heavy blanket in front of the fireplace. It shielded the light from the open door where he stood listening for the hoofbeats of Thomas Wiley's horse. In the corner of the room nearest the fireplace sat his wife Delilah, grief-stricken by the tragedy that had overtaken her sister.

As he waited, John wondered how he could break the news to Thomas. There was no way, he knew, to soften the blow. He would have to tell him at once and get it over with. At midnight he finally heard Thomas Wiley coming and went outside to meet him.

"Thomas!" he called. "Ride up to the house. There is . . . ." He hesitated. "There is something I must tell you."

Thomas Wiley sensed the urgency in John Borders' voice. Suddenly filled with anxiety, he turned off the path and rode toward the cabin.

"What's the trouble, John?" he asked. "What is it? Tell me. What is it?"

"The Indians have killed Jennie and the children. Batt Sellards, too," John said.

"The Indians have killed Jennie and the children," Thomas repeated, almost as if the words held no meaning.

"And burned your house," John added.

"And burned my house." The news was more than Thomas could take in. "I must go home, then. I must go home at once," he said. He could not believe what he had heard. He must see for himself.

John Borders knew what Thomas was thinking. "It *is* true, Thomas," he said gently. "I know. I have been there. I know, too, there is nothing you can do for Jennie and the children. By going there in the blackness of this terrible night, you may only bring about your own death."

"And if I did, what of it?" cried Thomas. "If Jennie and the children are gone, what have I to live for?"

"Wait until tomorrow and we will both go," said John.

At last Thomas dismounted and followed John to the house. The two rooms of the cabin were built with an open passageway between them, and here John tethered Thomas's horse. When the two men entered the cabin, John barred the heavy cabin door behind them, took down the heavy blanket which had shielded the firelight, and poked the fire. Then he persuaded Thomas to sit down, brought him hot food and drink, and tried to give him hope of finding Jennie. The two men spent the night talking, trying to figure out what must have happened, making plans for following the Indians.

As soon as the first streak of dawn appeared on the eastern horizon, Thomas and John set out for the scene of the massacre. Upon arriving at the half-burned cabin, they viewed for a moment the bodies of the children and Batt

33

Sellards, and then began a search for those of Jennie and her baby.

Within an hour or two many people had gathered. While Thomas and John continued their search for Jennie and little Tommy, friends and neighbors took care of the dead. The funeral service was held, and Hezekiah Sellards, as he often did when no minister was available, performed the funeral ceremony.

A careful search of the grounds around the cabin still revealed no evidence that Jennie and her baby had been murdered.

"I believe," said Thomas finally, "that Jennie and the baby have been taken as captives and that the Indians have probably taken them in the direction of New River."

"In that case," said John Borders, "we should be able to overtake them in two days of hard, fast riding."

Thomas Wiley was not an experienced Indian fighter. On some of his hunting trips with Tice Harman, he had been attacked by the Indians and had fought in some of the skirmishes that followed, but he knew little about following an Indian trail. That he lacked experience did not enter his mind at this time. His one idea was to rescue his wife and baby, and he believed he could do it if he could only overtake the Indians.

From the settlers he gathered together a pursuit party. Since most of the men were away from the settlement, the party consisted mostly of boys fifteen and sixteen years old. The youths carried whatever arms had been left at home by the hunters. All of them had hunting knives, and some of them carried guns.

Though only a few horses had been left by the hunting party, there were enough for each youth to have a mount. From the supply he had brought from the trading post, Thomas gave gunpowder and lead to those of the party

34

who had guns. When this had been done, they rode off into the forest in the direction of New River.

Six hours later Tice Harman and the hunters returned to the settlement. Swollen streams, bad crossings, and the heavy loads of skins and furs that their pack horses carried had delayed their progress.

Tice could hardly believe what he heard when, at his own cabin, he was told what had befallen the Wiley family, but it took him only a short time to figure out the exact course which the Indians had probably followed.

"At the point where our men could no longer follow their trail," he explained, "the Indians separated into two groups. These groups in turn separated into smaller groups. Some Indians, no doubt, traveled alone. This was done to throw us off their trail."

"It is my opinion," he continued, "that one group of Indians, carrying with them the body of the Cherokee prince, left immediately for the Indian villages north of the Ohio. Others, of course, came here to avenge the death of the chief's son."

At the scene of the massacre Tice Harman examined every detail. Footprints, bits of moss pressed more firmly to the rocks by moccasined feet, broken sticks, overturned stones, bits of thread that clung to thorns, all these and other clues Tice observed carefully. Believing he had picked up the trail, he rode off into the hills north of the cabin. His men waited near the Wiley cabin.

Two hours later he returned. "The Indians fled in the direction of the Bluestone River," he advised his men. "They have taken Jennie and the baby with them. The band is headed by the Cherokee chief. He is followed by ten Indians. They are traveling at an unbelievable rate of speed, considering the fact that Jennie must be carrying the baby in her arms."

36

The Indians had been on the march for about twenty-four hours, Tice believed, and were headed for the Tug River trail. "They will have to stop soon for a rest," he went on. "Sleep and rest are essential to hard marching. We can easily overtake them."

Tice calmed the fears of the settlers. "This is not a general uprising of the Indians," he said. "This mongrel band, made up, I am sure, of Indians from several tribes, was making one of its usual trips to the Cherokee villages in Tennessee. They happened upon our hunting camp quite by accident. The encounter was as much of a surprise to the Indians as it was to us. After the prince fell, the Cherokee chief made a dash for the settlement to avenge the death of his son. He has taken his revenge. The settlement need fear no further attacks. None will be made."

Tice picked ten of the most experienced Indian fighters in the Walker's Gap settlement. "These men will accompany me in pursuit of the Indians," he said. "We will leave at daybreak tomorrow. While we are gone, the other men will get everything ready so that we can leave for the Louisa River when we return. We must get a fort built there this winter."

"But what about Thomas Wiley?" asked Henry Skaggs. "He will want to join the search."

"Not if I can help it," Tice replied. "He is in no state of mind to go on a search of this kind. I hope that we can leave before he discovers that he is on the wrong track and returns from New River."

The next morning before daybreak Tice Harman and his ten picked fighters mounted the fleetest horses in the settlement and rode in the direction of the Bluestone River. They did not try to follow a trail, for although Tice well knew the trails that the Indians might take, he knew also the short cuts they were more likely to use.

FORCED MARCHING FOR JENNIE

On leaving the Wiley cabin, the Indians climbed the hill immediately to the north. It was steep and rough. It was broken by jagged rocks and cliffs. But the Indians seemed to find little difficulty in climbing it at great speed. The Cherokee chief led the way and set the pace. He leaped over fallen trees and boulders like a cat. He crawled through thickets of laurel and wild plum bushes.

Jennie found it difficult to keep up. With her child in her arms she could not pull herself up the cliffs by grasping at bushes or ledges of rock with both hands as the Indians did. But she did her best. She took long, fast steps in the darkness without knowing where she was going. She was guided

38

only by the movement of the Indian directly in front of her, whom she could hardly see in the darkness.

"Faster! Faster!" the Shawnee chief said repeatedly.

"I'll keep up," Jennie replied.

"War chief angry!" the Shawnee chief answered. "Papoose make White Squaw slow. War chief not like papoose."

"Don't let him touch my baby," Jennie pleaded.

"Faster then, faster," urged the Shawnee.

Jennie knew that, as a captive, she was the property of all the members of a band as long as the band was together. When the band separated, she would become the property of the Indian who had first laid hands on her. So, for the time being at least, she belonged to the band, not to the Shawnee chief who had claimed her as his captive. Any one of the band could kill her if he wished, and none of the others could do anything about it.

At the words of the Shawnee chief Jennie's heart sank within her. She would do her best to please them — yes, to please all of them.

"Oh, dear God, give me strength," she prayed.

As the night wore on, the darkness became deeper. Jennie's thoughts turned to her husband and to the neighbors she was leaving behind. She knew they would follow her as soon as they discovered that she and little Tommy were captives. They would try to rescue her. Marching was difficult in the black night, but marking the trail for others to follow was less likely to be noticed in the darkness than in the light of moon and stars. When she could do so without attracting the attention of the Shawnee chief, she broke off twigs from the bushes and dropped them in the path. She overturned stones. She left deep footprints in the earth in every spot soft enough for her to dig in her heels. She pulled out strands of her hair and dropped them in the path. And all the time, hardly knowing where she stepped, she kept on the heels of the Indian marching in front of her.

The Shawnee chief did a lot of talking. Whether he was talking to himself or to her, Jennie was not sure; but she realized that he was speaking in English and she heard enough of his conversation to get the importance of what he was saying.

"White Fawn — happy hunting ground," she heard him say. "White Fawn sew. White Squaw sew now. White Squaw make chief happy." From these words Jennie gathered that the chief's wife — or was White Fawn his daughter? — had gone to the happy hunting ground, and that she, White Squaw, was to take White Fawn's place.

When the Indians reached the top of the hill, they descended quickly on the other side. From there they crossed a narrow swamp where Jennie often sank in water and mud up to her knees.

Up the next mountain they climbed, and along the ridges. They seemed to be traveling with no particular direction in mind. Later Jennie learned that they knew, as if by instinct, just where to turn and just what path to take.

Jennie's long skirt of heavy linsey-woolsey material soaked up water like a sponge. When out of the water, it was soon half frozen and stiff. She was cold. The baby cried continuously at first, but after a while it nestled its chubby face in the curve of her neck and shoulder and sobbed only now and then. She patted its little shoulders. This comforted both of them.

By taking short cuts rather than the well-worn trails, the Indians had shortened by half the distance from the Wiley cabin to the head of Walker's Creek. Midnight found them between Wolf Creek and Bluestone River. Here they stopped in the shelter of a large rockhouse.

The old Shawnee chief indicated by a motion of the hand that Jennie was to sit down and rest.

She sat down on the dry sand and drew an easy breath for the first time since setting out from the cabin. Her dog Tige, who had followed her without any protest from the Indians, crept up beside her and lay down at her feet.

From somewhere in the darkness, perhaps from a crack in the rocks, a Wyandotte warrior produced two pieces of flint, some dry punk, and dry leaves. With these he started a fire. The other Indians added twigs and sticks. As the fire caught, they piled on branches and then huge pieces of logs. Soon a big fire was going.

The Cherokee warrior who had taken the life of Batt Sellards untied the thongs by which the pack on his back had been fastened and laid the pack upon the floor of the rockhouse. He unfolded the leather flaps and took from the pack several pieces of lean venison. These he distributed in equal amounts, first to each of the Indians and then to Jennie. The Indians cut long sticks on the creek bank nearby and sharpened the ends. On the pointed sticks they fastened the venison, which they held above the flames to broil. When it was done, they sat in a circle about the great fire, eating the broiled venison and seeming to enjoy it.

The Shawnee broiled some venison and handed it to Jennie.

"Eat," he said.

Jennie took the venison and ate as much of it as she could. She did not like its taste, but it gave her nourishment that she needed. She tried to give her baby some venison, too, for she knew that he must be hungry and that he needed nourishment just as she did, but little Tommy turned his head and refused to eat.

41

Outside, the rain had now turned to snow. The wind was blowing. The weather was getting much colder. While it was still quite dark, the Indians put out the fire. They tried to conceal all trace of it by burying the ashes in the sand. Then they took up the march again.

As before, the Cherokee chief led the way. Jennie was the eleventh person in line. Her clothing had dried. She had rested. The broiled venison had provided some nourishment. She felt refreshed and more equal than before to the marching ahead of her. The Shawnee chief marched behind her.

"Faster!" he urged. Always his words were, "Faster! Faster!"

Daylight found the marchers at the head of the Bluestone River. The creeks and branches were full to overflowing. Often the marchers were in water up to their armpits. The water was cold, but that did not keep the Indians from wading streams as they came to them. They waded the smaller streams from their sources to their junction with the larger streams. This was to leave no trail that could be followed.

Jennie found it difficult to keep up with the Indians when wading the streams. Her long skirt, now torn in many places, was a hindrance to her. Her heavy shoes slowed her progress through the mud and the loose, wet sand of the streams. Hard as she tried to keep up, the Cherokee chief often seemed displeased and shouted, "Kill White Squaw. Kill papoose!"

The Shawnee chief had noticed that Jennie was marking the trail, and now he watched her at all times. If she overturned a stone, even by accident, he warned, "War chief kill!"

The marching had been fast the night before, but it did not compare with the speed of daylight marching. The

42

Indians never seemed to tire. They carried themselves straight, their shoulders back. Each put his foot exactly in the track of the Indian who preceded him. Most followers of the trail would have thought only one Indian had gone that way.

They crossed the beautiful Great Flat Top Mountain. Giant trees stood leafless in the November breeze. Wild fowl flew from one tree to another as the guard bird called out warning of the approach of an enemy. Bears and deer were frequently seen, but the Indians did not disturb them. They killed game only when they needed it for food or for skins and furs.

From Great Flat Top Mountain, the Indians traveled south along the ridge between the Guyandot and the Tug rivers. They were on an old trail and seemed wholly familiar with their surroundings.

43

THE SECOND NIGHT IN CAPTIVITY

The Cherokee chief stopped under the overhanging roof of a huge rockhouse and gave the Indians directions to make camp. The order was met with cries which sounded to Jennie like "O-oh-yo-o! O-oh-yo-o!" and which seemed to be cries of pleasure.

The Wyandotte warrior who had started the fire the night before again found flint rocks and dry punk in some hidden spot. The other Indians brought branches of trees from the forest and soon, as before, a big fire was going.

44

The Indians seemed relaxed and happy, and Jennie guessed that they were no longer afraid of being overtaken by a rescue party. This worried her considerably, for she had hoped that someone from the settlement would take up the pursuit at once. She felt sure that John Borders would return to her cabin after she failed to arrive at his house, and she knew that Thomas would be home from the trading post that same night. "Surely," she thought, "somebody started in pursuit of us before morning."

The Cherokee warrior, who had provided the only food Jennie had had since she had been taken captive, again took dried venison from his pack and gave it out in equal amounts to each member of the band. Jennie accepted her portion gratefully, for she realized that she must eat to keep up her strength.

"Thank you," she said to the Cherokee. "Thank you very much."

The Cherokee looked at her and muttered. Gratitude, evidently, was something the Indians knew nothing about.

Each Indian held his dried venison above the flames until it was cooked. Jennie did likewise, but she did not enjoy the meat. Without salt it was worse than tasteless. It made her almost sick.

The Shawnee chief drew a wallet from the bosom of his shirt. He took from it some parched corn which he handed to Jennie. "Eat!" he said.

She took the corn, thanked him, as she had thanked the Cherokee for the venison, and ate. The parched corn tasted pleasant to her after the unsavory dried venison and she felt better.

During the twenty-four hours she had been on the march Jennie had traveled many more miles than she had ever traveled in a similar length of time. She had suffered more from exposure than she had ever suffered in her whole life.

She had waded swift streams of icy water up to her armpits. She had climbed over jagged rocks and cliffs during the blackness of the night with little more than instinct to guide her. She had grasped at trees and ledges which she could not see. She had leaped ditches, as the Indian in front of her had done, without knowing their width or depth. She had descended steep precipices. She had crawled through thickets of mountain laurel and wild crab apple. Her clothing had been badly torn. Her legs had been cut and scratched by rocks, thorns, and brambles. Her feet were sore and blistered. But in spite of all the hardships, she had kept the pace set by the Cherokee chief. For the present, at least, she had saved her own life and Tommy's life.

But little Tommy was in great distress. He had cried until he was too hoarse to cry any more. He, too, had been drenched to the skin. He had been cold. He wheezed when he breathed. He refused to eat.

46

Jennie held him close to her and patted his back and shoulders. "My baby," she said. "My darling baby."

He was so little and helpless. How could he possibly survive the cold and the exposure? Jennie hardly dared to think about it.

"God be merciful to an innocent child," she prayed.

The Indians relaxed before the big fire. They, too, were tired from the continuous marching, but they were not suffering from it as Jennie and the baby were, because they were used to it. They talked very little. There was no laughter. Each one amused himself in his own way until it was time for sleep.

Before lying down around the great fire for sleep and rest, the Indians bound Jennie with narrow strips of deerskin. Her legs were tied tightly at the ankles and knees so that she could not move them. Her arms were pulled behind her until her elbows touched, and were tied in that position. Her wrists, too, were tied so tightly that she could not move one upon the other.

The baby was left to lie upon the ground beside her, but, tied as she was, she could do nothing to comfort him. His wheezing continued, and he cried feverishly, so that Jennie, in addition to her own suffering and pain, felt all the agony of a mother who can give her child no help in his distress.

After Jennie was tied up, the Indians lay down in a circle around the fire, like spokes in a great wheel. They all lay with their feet toward the fire and their knees drawn up toward the chin. Soon they were fast asleep.

Jennie, however, could not go to sleep, nor could she rest. Her whole body felt bruised and beaten. Her ankles and wrists began to swell under the tightly tied strips of deerskin until the thongs cut into the flesh with almost unbearable pain. Her muscles ached and, worst of all, she could not keep from her mind the dreadful thoughts of all that had happened. Every time she closed her eyes she saw again the upraised tomahawks, heard the war whoops of the Indians and the splintering crash of the cabin door. Events crowded into her mind until she cried aloud with the remembered horror.

Her cries awakened the old Shawnee chief who lay upon the ground beside her. He looked at her and knew that she was running a high fever. He arose to a sitting position. He took a knife from its sheath and, as gently as he could, he cut the strips of deerskin with which she was bound. This gave her the freedom of movement she needed, but she was still in great distress. She continued to cry out and to toss feverishly.

By the dim light of the slowly dying fire, the old chief watched her as she tossed from side to side. From her cries

48

he knew that the white squaw who was to take the place of White Fawn was in great pain and that her condition was serious enough to need care and attention. He got up, lighted a torch, and walked out into the forest.

Some minutes later he returned, carrying four different kinds of leaves. These he pressed into an earthenware vessel which he had taken from his pack. He filled the vessel with water and set it on the red embers, where it simmered until the liquid had become dark brown. Then he took it off the fire and stirred the liquid until it was cool enough to drink. He held up Jennie's head with one hand and put the vessel to her lips with the other.

"Drink!" he said.

The liquid was bitter, but he made her swallow it. Again and again he forced her to swallow, until all the contents of the cup were gone. Then he said, "Sleep!"

A moment later Jennie dropped off into sleep. She continued to be restless, but she did not awaken again until, in the morning, she heard the Shawnee chief saying, "Go! Go!"

He was shaking her by the shoulders. There was gentleness in his manner, but Jennie knew there was no time to lose. The Cherokee chief was always impatient. She rubbed her eyes and then, reaching for her baby, she took him in her arms. She held her ear against his chest. His heart was still beating; he was still breathing.

"God be praised," she said half aloud.

The Shawnee chief gave her some venison prepared in the same manner as on previous occasions. This she ate. Then he gave her some parched corn, which she chewed until it was soft and gave to the baby. She was greatly pleased when he swallowed it. Now, when the time came, she could set forth on the journey, for now she had hopes that her baby would live.

INDIAN THREATS

The Cherokee chief sat in front of the fire for several minutes without speaking. Jennie was fearful of what he might be thinking, for he seemed troubled. At length he got up and walked to a large rock outside the rockhouse. He sat down upon it and called to the Indians.

One by one the other Indians left their positions around the campfire and went to the chief. They seated themselves in a semicircle in front of him, as they always did when a council was held. They crossed their feet in front of them and held their knees with their hands. The chief did most of the talking. The other Indians frequently said something in unison and nodded their heads in approval.

Jennie could not be sure what the council was about, but she strongly suspected that it had to do with the possibility of being overtaken by the men from the settlement. The words "Tice Harman," "White Squaw," and "papoose" occurred again and again, and often the Indians made gestures in her direction which were anything but friendly.

"How I wish the men from the settlement would come!" she said to herself. "What has delayed them?"

She knew she could not continue for long the fast marching pace that was set each day by the Cherokee chief. She was tired. She was cut, scratched, and bruised. Her feet were sore and blistered. Her muscles ached. She was fearful both for herself and for the baby.

She was certain that Thomas Wiley would come to her rescue. She knew that Tice Harman would come, too, for Tice Harman and Thomas Wiley, in spite of the difference in their ages, were almost like brothers.

Thomas Wiley had come from Scotland to settle in America ten years ago. On his arrival in Virginia, he had joined a number of other persons who were also setting out to make homes for themselves in the wilderness. It was Tice who guided this band of new settlers to lands suitable for their homes. He and Thomas Wiley had been friends from the first, and Tice, the older by almost twenty years, had taken the younger man under his wing.

For the first two years, Thomas Wiley had lived at the home of Tice Harman. He had lived there during the time of his courtship of Jennie. It was to his home that Thomas had taken her after their wedding. And it was there they had both lived while Thomas Wiley was building their own cabin on the land he had bought from Tice Harman. Tice was their closest friend and nearest neighbor. Yes, Tice Harman would come to her rescue, she was sure. But when? Oh, when would he come?

When the council was over the Indians rose to their feet. Each one of them made motions of agreement with his hands and arms and mumbled something which seemed to be words of approval. Then two of them disappeared into the blackness of the forest.

The Cherokee chief gave orders to the others to put out the fire, to bury the ashes, and to conceal, as far as possible, every trace of the overnight camping. If they could help it,

51

the Indians never left any sign of their presence anywhere at any time.

After his orders had been obeyed, the Cherokee chief again took his place at the head of the line of march, and the other Indians fell into the positions they had taken on the previous days of marching. Before the sun was yet up, they continued their journey.

The mountain streams, filled to overflowing from the almost continuous rainfall of the past forty-eight hours, were swift and treacherous. The ground in the lowlands was under water. This made marching so slow and hazardous that the Indians took to the ridges as much as possible. The hills were high, rocky, and steep. Cliffs, jagged rocks, and boulders stood like sentinels to block passage, but the Indians were used to this kind of traveling and nothing held them back.

Jennie, with the baby in her arms, made every effort to keep up. Time and time again she called upon every bit of her strength, but she could not make her way so quickly and skillfully as the Indians did. The Shawnee chief often kept her from stumbling, but the other Indians gave her no help at all. Instead, they complained constantly about her slowness, and now and again they threatened to kill her child. The Shawnee chief always protested, and so the Indians were continually quarreling and arguing about her among themselves.

Jennie was young and strong. She had always lived an outdoor life, helping Thomas Wiley clear the forests, tend the crops, and gather the harvests. She had helped him dig ginseng in summer and run the trap lines in winter. With faith and courage she had met the privations of pioneer life and accustomed her body to toil and hardship. But this experience was beyond anything she had ever had to endure, and she began to show signs of weakness. At best, her

52

strength was hardly equal to that of the Indians and she needed still greater strength in order to carry the baby. When she showed signs of faltering, the threats upon her life were renewed.

"Kill White Squaw," the Cherokee chief often shouted.

"Faster! Faster!" the Shawnee chief then urged.

"Kill White Squaw! Faster! Faster!" How the words kept running through her mind!

About an hour before sunset, the Indians came to another rockhouse. The Cherokee chief indicated that camp was to be made for the night. Although Jennie did not wholly understand his words, she understood his meaning, and the order to stop was good news. Her strength was almost gone. She doubted that she could have kept going for another hour. Tommy's condition had grown steadily worse during the day, and Jennie's one thought was of how she could make him more comfortable. She was thankful, therefore, to have a few hours when she could care for the needs of her baby and rest her own weary body.

A black bear had been sighted a short distance from the rockhouse, and a Wyandotte warrior was sent to kill it. It was not long before he returned with the carcass of the slain animal.

The Indians removed the skin from the carcass and cut the meat into quarters. Then they cut the quarters into thin slices, which they broiled over the campfire. They spent most of the night feasting. They ate and ate and ate until they could eat no more.

This gave Jennie hope of a few hours' rest at least for, knowing the habits of the Indians, she remembered that they ate little while marching and much when they expected to spend some time in leisure. But her anxiety about little Tommy was greater than ever, for he seemed to be getting sicker and sicker. He was hot and feverish, it was hard for him to breathe, and his little cries of distress were weak and hoarse. The Shawnee chief, noticing her anxiety, listened to the child's breathing. Then he melted some of the bear fat in a small earthenware pot which he carried for the brewing of his medicines. He gave the warm bear fat to Jennie and told her to rub the child's chest with it.

After Jennie had done this, she got Tommy to swallow some of the melted fat. The treatment seemed to be just what he needed. He began to breathe more easily and the warm bear fat that he swallowed seemed to give his little body strength.

"God be praised!" said the thankful Jennie.

The old Shawnee, acting now as medicine man rather than as chief, turned his attention to Jennie, for he saw that her feet and ankles were badly swollen.

He took a leather bag from his shirt and disappeared into the forest. He was gone only a short time, but when he returned, he had a great collection of leaves, roots, and barks. These he mixed in the earthenware pot with the inner layers of the bark of the white oak tree, and then set the pot on the fire to boil. As soon as the mixture had been boiled until it was quite thick, he took it off the fire and set it upon the ground to cool.

When the mixture was not too hot, he had Jennie bathe her feet in it. Its healing effect was amazing. The swelling soon disappeared, and so did almost all of the pain. Then the chief, telling her to use the mixture again later, left her to herself.

54

When the night was far spent, the Indians stopped their feasting. They lay down around the fire in the same positions as on the previous night, and were soon fast asleep.

Since Jennie had not been bound with leather thongs as before, she was free to take care of her child. She rubbed his chest again with the warm, melted fat, and again it seemed to make him comfortable. Then she bathed her own feet again. They no longer hurt her and she felt more at peace than she had for days. She knelt beside Tommy and thanked God for His loving kindness and tender mercy. Then she lay down beside the child and, a moment later, dropped off into a deep, untroubled sleep.

The Indians were up at break of day, as was their custom. But Jennie slept on, and the Shawnee chief let her sleep as long as he dared to. He had bad news for her. She would need all the strength she could gather to bear it.

At last the time came when he had to awaken her. He shook her gently by the shoulders until she opened her eyes. Seeing the compassionate face of the Indian chief she smiled a little, and put out her hand to touch her baby.

"No," said the chief, who knew what it was to lose a child. "No. He is not there."

Jennie sat up with a cry and looked around her, unable to believe what she feared.

"They didn't — . They didn't — ." She could not finish the sentence.

"No," said the Shawnee. "No — papoose safe from Cherokee now."

"Safe!" exclaimed Jennie. "You mean — ?" and then suddenly she knew, from the look on the Shawnee's face, what he did mean. "Oh, no, no, no," she cried. "And I slept! I slept! How could I?"

"I took care," said the Shawnee. "Papoose too sick. Papoose go like White Fawn."

55

Jennie buried her face in her hands and wept. To lose the last of her children seemed more than she could bear. Then the words of the Shawnee went through her mind, "Papoose safe from Cherokee now." It was true. Jennie wiped her eyes and said a prayer. "God give me strength," she prayed. "Thy will, not mine, be done."

When she lifted her head from prayer, the Shawnee took her hand and helped her to her feet. White Squaw was a brave woman. He had known it from the beginning.

He had her bathe her feet in the liquid again. Then they both took their places in the line of march. Without a word and scarcely a look from the Cherokee, they began the third day's journey.

ANOTHER DAY OF MARCHING

Heavy rains had fallen during the night. The small streams had again overflowed their banks. They were swift, deep, and treacherous. The lowlands were filled with water, mud, and quicksands. Because of these conditions the Cherokee chief said they would take to the ridges. The other Indians shouted words of approval. Their line of march was now along the range of mountains that extended in the general direction of the Ohio River.

Jennie felt better able to keep the pace set by the Cherokee chief than on the previous morning. Her feet and ankles were no longer swollen, and their soreness had almost disappeared. Though her heart was heavy, she made up her mind to keep up with the Indians at any cost, praying that they would spare her life until rescue came. The thought of returning to her husband still gave her something to hope for and to live for.

Rain continued to fall. At times it came down in torrents. The wind swept it around the mountainside in great white sheets. The Indians were forced many times to take shelter beneath overhanging rocks on the mountainsides and the ridges. This was a great help to Jennie. Each stop gave her a chance to rest and to catch her breath. Each time that she took up the march, it was with renewed determination to keep up with the pace set.

The old Shawnee chief was pleased with her marching. "White Squaw good Indian," he said to her.

As on previous days, he helped her over steep places, steadied her when she stumbled or tripped, and did all that he could to make marching easier for her.

The Cherokee chief gave her no encouragement or sign of approval, though Jennie knew he could not help but notice that she was doing better. Now that Tommy was gone, she thought, probably he would be satisfied only when he could be rid of her, too. Sooner or later, she feared, he would find an excuse to end her life. She would postpone that fateful moment as long as possible by causing as little delay as she could. She would keep up.

The downpour of rain continued. It was accompanied by a terrific windstorm, which uprooted some trees and tore branches off others. The Indians, as well as Jennie, were wet to the skin. They were cold and shivering. At length the Cherokee chief gave orders to take shelter in a small rockhouse.

To this the other Indians agreed readily. The flint rocks, the dry punk, and the dry leaves were produced as on other occasions, and soon a great, blazing fire was going. Its warmth and comfort were enjoyed by every member of the band.

The bear slayer opened his pack. He took from it huge chunks of lean bear meat, which he cut into thin strips and distributed in equal portions to each member of the party. Jennie broiled her portion in the usual manner, but she could scarcely force herself to chew it, and she found it harder still to swallow. For four days she had had no nourishment but unsavory bits of dried venison, fresh bear meat,

58

and a few kernels of parched corn. Her stomach simply rebelled at the sight of more food of this kind.

The Indians who had been sent on scouting duty that morning returned shortly after dark. The report they gave was entirely in their native tongue, but Jennie guessed that it contained good news for the Indians, for they showed signs of being pleased. The Cherokee chief had listened in a happier frame of mind than on the other occasions when a council had been held. Could it be, Jennie asked herself, that Thomas had been unable to pick up their trail?

After they had heard the report, the Indians lay down in their usual positions around the fire. The Shawnee chief lay on one side of Jennie and a Shawnee warrior on the other.

Again Jennie was not bound. She was in less pain than on previous nights, but she could not keep her mind from thoughts and fears of the future. Would she be able to stand another day of hard marching? She did not know. To attempt escape at this time would bring certain death to her, she was sure. She could not sleep. She could not keep the thought of little Tommy's death out of her mind. She turned and tossed from one side to the other. She could hardly control the trembling of her body.

Long before daylight the Cherokee was up giving orders for departure.

This was followed by the usual words of approval from the other Indians, and soon they were off for another day of hard marching through the hills of West Virginia. They were still traveling in the general direction of the Ohio.

Upon leaving camp that morning, Jennie had felt really ill. She had been unable to take the nourishment she needed. Her strength was failing. She made every effort to keep up, but found it almost impossible.

"Faster!" warned the Shawnee. "Faster! War chief kill White Squaw!"

"I'll do my best," Jennie replied.

In the early afternoon the two scouts, who had again been sent back that morning to make sure there was no pursuit party on their trail, returned. They reported that they were being followed by men on horseback.

The Cherokee chief held a council meeting. He stood and talked while the other Indians sat in a semicircle about him. One of the Delawares suggested that the chief should remain behind and ambush Tice Harman.

But the Cherokee did not agree with the plan proposed. He knew that Tice Harman was as crafty as an Indian. He knew that such a plan was as likely to end in his own death as in the death of the white man. Instead of waiting in ambush he proposed that White Squaw, who was slowing up their progress, be killed, and that they change their course.

The old Shawnee chief once more came to her rescue. "White Squaw live," he said. "White Squaw keep up."

"Ugh! Ugh! Ugh!" shouted the Cherokee angrily. But he gave the order to fall in line, and the party, traveling at a much greater rate of speed than before, proceeded in the direction of Tug River.

Each time that she set her foot down, Jennie tried to put it in the track left by the Indian in front of her, but she just couldn't reach it. Neither could she step as fast as the Indians were stepping.

The small streams emptying into Tug River were not so full of water as were the streams they had come to the day before. Consequently the Indians again changed their tactics. They no longer followed the ridges, but they waded the streams instead. When the water in one stream was too deep for wading, they looked for another. They seemed to be more concerned about leaving no trail behind them than they were in covering distance.

60

Jennie was not equal to wading. When the bottom was soft, she could hardly pull one foot out of the mud and place it ahead of the other. In spite of all she could do, she fell behind.

"Faster! Faster!" the Shawnee chief warned continuously. "Faster! Faster, White Squaw, faster!"

Jennie tried, but without success. The continual warnings, the fear in her heart, the dreadful suspense, all these almost overcame her in her struggle to keep up.

The Cherokee chief stopped the line of march and waded back from his place at the front toward Jennie. Realizing from the look in his eyes that her last moment was near, Jennie did the only thing she could think of. She ran out of the stream and with suddenly renewed strength fled into the forest.

"No!" shouted the astonished Shawnee chief. "No, White Squaw, no!"

But Jennie did not stop. She raced ahead with all her might. The Shawnee chief ran after her. He managed always to stay between her and the Cherokee chief who was close behind. At last he caught up with her. He seized her right arm above the wrist and, holding it up in the grip of his powerful left hand, he faced the Cherokee chief.

The Cherokee uttered a cry that sounded like the snarl of a defeated animal and lowered his tomahawk. Once more the Shawnee had saved Jennie's life by claiming her as his prisoner. But after all that she had gone through, this last cruel suspense was more than Jennie could stand. The world turned black before her and she fainted. When she regained consciousness some minutes later, she was lying on the ground near the stream she had been wading. The Shawnee chief was bathing her temples with water.

When Jennie could again stand on her feet, she saw that she must resume her position in the line of march. In some strange way she knew, as surely as though it were a message from heaven, that her life was no longer in danger from the Cherokee. With the dread of him lifted from her heart and mind, she marshaled her strength to meet whatever hardships the days ahead might bring.

There would be no more suffering for little Tommy. For that, at least, she felt that she must be thankful. And dear to her though Tommy had been, she found that, without him in her arms, it was easier for her to wade the streams and climb the difficult trails. Now that she could grasp at shrubs and branches with both hands, she could pull herself up the cliffs and mountains which otherwise might well have been insurmountable.

She seemed to have renewed strength, too. She did not know why, but after each ordeal she was better able, it seemed, to face the next one. Perhaps it was all part of a divine plan.

It was growing dark when the party reached Tug River at a point a short distance below the meeting of Marrowbone Creek with the river. Ordinarily narrow and shallow at this point, Tug River was now a sea of water between the mountain ridges on either side. In the middle of the stream drifted treetops, logs, and other debris which the angry waters had picked up when they had overflowed the banks of the narrow stream. The sea of water seemed even wilder and more violent because a thunderstorm was raging. Zigzag streaks of lightning flashed across the black sky, and great sheets of white lightning lighted up the whole countryside. Thunder, such as one expects to hear only in July and August, roared through the valley, echoing and re-echoing in the hills and gorges.

The Cherokee chief, undaunted by the angry waters, ordered the Indians to swim the swollen river. The order was met by shouts of approval and the Indians began to adjust their packs, bows, and arrows for swimming.

Jennie backed away from the water.

"No! White Squaw, no!" shouted the Shawnee chief. "Swim river!"

Though swimming in swift water had been a part of Jennie's backwoods education, she was reluctant to enter this raging flood. Besides, guessing from the behavior of the Indians that the rescue party was not far away, she hated to put this angry stream between her and her friends. But the Indians were in no mood for delay. Two of the warriors grabbed her by the arms and dragged her to the water's edge. She dug her heels in the mud. She pulled back.

"Ugh! Ugh!" shouted the warriors. "White Squaw swim."

They squatted to dive. As they made the leap, the Cherokee chief gave Jennie a hard shove.

"No! No! Let me —" But Jennie's sentence was not finished. She felt the ice-cold water surge over her body. When she came to the surface, she took a deep breath and prepared to strike out for the other shore, realizing that she must make headway now or death by drowning would be her doom.

Scarcely had the last Indian in the band touched the current in midstream when Tice Harman and his picked fighters came to the bank which the Indians had just left. In bright flashes of lightning they could see the swimmers. One man lifted his gun to his shoulder.

64

"No!" said Tice Harman. "Don't shoot!"

"Why not?" asked the man. "We can't miss."

"If we shoot, they will drown Jennie," said Tice. "We must take no chances on that."

Tice and his men tethered their horses to the bushes where they could not be seen by the Indians. Then, keeping under cover, they slipped along the bank of the river and watched the crossing.

The Indians swam in an almost upright position. With one on either side of her, Jennie found swimming for herself impossible. She could not use her legs as a swimmer usually does, and her arms were held by her captors. But she scarcely needed to do more than relax and let the Indians do the swimming for her as well as for themselves. They used their free hands merely to guide their bodies, as they let the swift current carry them through the water. They avoided logs and steered themselves around treetops. With a skill that was uncanny, they kept themselves from being caught in the river debris that rushed past them.

These three — the white woman and her two captors — were carried down the river for what, to Jennie, seemed miles. The other Indians swam in the water near them. Not a word was spoken by anyone. Flashes of lightning helped them to see one another and to stay close together. At last they reached the west side of the river at the mouth of a small creek.

As they were carried into the mouth of the creek, they found themselves in deep, still water. Here, where there was no swift current to carry them along in their upright position, it was difficult for the Indians to progress and at the same time to keep their captive's head above water. But after a struggle, they reached the far side of the creek and as soon as they touched the bank, they released Jennie.

"Sit down," commanded the Shawnee chief, and Jennie did not wait for a second command. She was completely exhausted.

One by one the other Indians made safe landings. As each reached the shore, he, too, sat down upon the ground.

On the opposite side of the river Tice Harman and his picked fighters lay hidden in the grasses. When the last Indian had been seated, Tice said to his men, "We'll take 'em in the morning."

66

Tice Harman and his men made camp that night with the determination to "take 'em in the morning." But the old Cherokee chief had no intention of being taken. He planned to lose no time in going forward.

Not far from where he sat, a small stream flowed down the steep mountainside. Its bottom was of shale, which at times was very slippery, but it provided a path for the Indians to take. There would be no tracks left in the water. So up the steep and swift mountain stream they waded. Often Jennie slipped, lost her footing, and fell face forward in the rushing waters. Drenched again and again in the icy stream, she still managed to pick herself up each time and go forward.

By the time the top of the mountain was reached, there had been a change in the weather. The electrical storm was over. Stars appeared in the sky. The wind was blowing. It was much colder.

"Cold weather good," the Shawnee chief said to Jennie. "Indians march faster."

"God forbid," thought Jennie, but she made no answer that he could hear.

From the top of the mountain the Indians kept on down the steep slopes into the next valley. The way down was so much easier than the struggle to climb up the other side had been that Jennie felt almost rested when she reached the foot of the mountain. The country round about seemed to be familiar to the Indians. They headed straight for a rock-house which was apparently already known to them. Here, at the command of the Cherokee chief, they rested.

67

Far back from the opening of the rockhouse, in a passage-way that seemed to lead still farther back into the mountain, a fire was kindled. Although the light could scarcely be seen from the outside, the Indians stood between the fire and the entrance of the rockhouse. In this manner, they shielded the glow cast by the flickering fire from anyone who might be passing by.

The night was already far spent, but to the Cherokee chief the importance of continuing the march was greater than the need for sleep. When the Indians were warmed and rested, he gave the order to resume the march. They shouted the usual words of approval and set out, this time in the direction of the Louisa River.

Although they had scarcely eaten since the night-long feast on bear meat, they were in good marching condition. Jennie herself felt somewhat stronger and better able to keep up with them. Even the old Cherokee chief no longer found fault with her marching. By midafternoon, they sighted the Louisa River.

On the march, deer and other animals had been seen in the lowlands, and the Cherokee chief now sent one of his warriors to kill a deer for a feast.

68

Jennie watched the warrior crawl noiselessly through the grasses and the bushes. Keeping himself downwind from the deer, he moved as quietly as a cat until he was within a few paces of the beautiful animal. Then he knelt on his left knee and aimed an arrow. Its flight was perfect. The graceful animal dropped to its knees and rolled over on its side. While it still breathed, the Cherokee ran to it and, with its head in his arms, spoke the prayer that all Indians must speak before the spirit of the deer leaves its body.

"Little Deer," he prayed, "forgive me for killing. Indians need meat."

Jennie could not hear the words, but she knew the Indian belief that he who kills a deer must ask its spirit, the Little Deer, to forgive him before it takes its flight from the body. Otherwise the spirit will go immediately to the hunter's home to await his return and to inflict sickness on his body for the rest of his life.

After the prayer had been said, the slain animal was carried to a small rockhouse nearby. There it was dressed and cut into thin slices, which the Indians broiled over the fire that had been started.

The Shawnee chief insisted that Jennie eat her full share of the lean venison. "White Squaw need food," he said. "White Squaw eat."

"Thank you," Jennie replied. Although she was almost too tired to be hungry, she knew she needed nourishment. And so she ate the broiled venison and found it good.

When the Indians had eaten and rested, the old Cherokee chief, who for several hours had been restless and uneasy, insisted that the march be continued.

"Cover fire," he said. "Bury ashes."

When all signs of their fires had been obliterated, the Indians headed for the banks of the Louisa River. The Louisa, like the Tug, had overflowed its banks, and its current was swift, its waters deep. Knowing that they must cross, the Indians plunged into the river, two of them taking Jennie as they had before. Daylight and fair weather made swimming seem easy. After crossing the current in midstream, the two Indians released Jennie to do her own swimming, and she reached the opposite bank by herself.

Cold and soaking wet though they were, the Indians did not halt when they reached dry ground but headed straight for the hills. Late that night they came to a secluded rock-house, and here the Cherokee chief said, "Stop. We stay here. We sleep!"

Soon the Wyandotte had a big fire going. The Indians stood or sat around it, getting themselves warm and dry. All seemed relieved of worry and perfectly at ease. Even the old Cherokee chief, now that he had put two treacherous rivers between him and the white men, had lost his uneasiness and his concern about being followed. When they were thoroughly dry and comfortable, the Indians lay down in their usual manner and slept until morning.

Jennie was weary but not completely exhausted. For the first time since her captivity had begun, she felt relaxed

70

and soon she, too, went to sleep and slept without waking until morning.

For once the Indians did not rise till long after the sun was up, though occasionally during the night one of them did get up to put more wood on the fire. As soon as he had done this, he lay down and slept again without waking the others.

About midmorning, the old Cherokee chief woke his sleeping companions, for it was time to think about eating. There were buffalo in the canebrakes nearby, and buffalo meat would make a feast for them. The Cherokee warrior and a Wyandotte were sent to the canebrakes.

Within an hour, they had returned to the rockhouse with the choice parts of a large buffalo. The meat was cut into thin strips as the meat had been cut on previous occasions. It was then distributed among the members of the party in equal amounts as usual.

The Indians broiled the buffalo meat over the flames just as they had broiled the bear meat and the venison. They ate until they could eat no more. Jennie, amazed at the great quantity that one Indian could consume, had noticed that after they had gorged themselves with food, the Indians never did any work. They rested and slept and stored up energy for days of marching when they would eat only enough food to satisfy the pangs of hunger. So in this case, after the feast they lay down and slept until the sun was sinking behind the western hills.

The days following the feast of buffalo meat were spent in a leisurely manner. The Indians went on their way, but there were no more forced marches. They hunted, marched, fished, or rested according to their mood. Danger of pursuit was so far behind them that they no longer worried about being overtaken. On the ninth day of the march, they reached the banks of the Ohio River.

DEPARTURE OF THE CHEROKEE

The Indians reached the Ohio River near the point where the Louisa River empties into it. Both rivers were overflowing their banks. Backwater from the Louisa and from the smaller streams flowing into the Ohio had spread over the lowlands. As far as the eye could see, there was nothing but muddy, debris-covered water.

The current in midstream was swift. Great drifts of logs, broken treetops, brushwood, and other debris had been caught up by the flood and were floating downstream. In the stiller waters on either side of the swift current, the tops of willows, sycamores, and birch trees, swaying in the breeze, showed the great depth of the water.

The Indians were surprised and disappointed to find the Ohio so flooded. Nevertheless, they were happy to be as close as they were to the Indian villages on its north bank. Looking out upon the turbulent waters, they repeated over and over again the name which means Beautiful River, "O-hi-yo! O-hi-yo! O-hi-yo!"

72

The Shawnee chief alone seemed dejected. He alone failed to call out, "O-hi-yo! O-hi-yo! O-hi-yo!" Instead, he gazed toward the north and pointing to the north bank of the Ohio River said to Jennie, "Over there live the Shawnees. Over there, White Squaw become Shawnee chief's daughter. Then White Squaw marry Shawnee warrior."

But until the Indians reached the Shawnee villages and the captive had been released by the band to her captor, the chief's plans could not be carried out. According to Indian ritual, the adoption ceremony must come first. This was a formal affair which lasted for days. It could be performed only in the presence of the whole tribe. So no matter how great was the desire of the chief to make Jennie his adopted daughter and to give her in marriage to one of his warriors, he would have to wait until the river had subsided and they could reach the other side.

The Cherokee chief, who was looking the situation over, also decided that the river was too wide and too deep to swim. He turned and ordered the Indians to make for the hills and ridges along the south bank of the Ohio. This they did, and for several days proceeded west along the banks of the muddy river. Each day they hoped the waters would recede to the point where it would be safe to try to swim the river. When they reached the bank of Little Sandy, they found this stream, too, overflowing its channel and the lowlands on either side filled with backwater. At this the Indians seemed perplexed and uncertain.

The Cherokee chief called a meeting of the council. The meeting lasted for some time. Jennie could only guess what it was about but she did not think her own fate was being discussed, for the Indians seldom looked in her direction.

Toward the end of the meeting, the two scouts who had been sent back to spy upon the pursuit party rejoined the band. Jennie did not hear the report they made, but she guessed that it contained good news for the Indians. They danced and shouted and seemed more at ease than at any time since the march had begun.

Later Jennie was to learn what had actually happened. Tice Harman and his men had swum their horses across the Tug River the morning after they had watched the crossing by the Indians. Expecting to overtake Jennie's captors in the hills nearby, they had been greatly disappointed to find that the Indians had not made camp the night before. After considerable effort, they had been able to pick up the trail which, again to their disappointment, led to the Louisa. Here Tice had said to his men, "The Cherokee chief has outwitted us. He has crossed the Louisa and is headed for the Ohio. We'll never be able to overtake him now."

His men had agreed, and the pursuit party had then returned to Walker's Gap. Here they had told the settlers that they had found the body of little Tommy and given it decent burial, wrapping it in a hunting jacket and burying it in a grave on high, dry land. They had rolled huge stones on the grave to prevent wild animals from molesting it. Afterwards, they said, they had seen Jennie Wiley swim the river, and an examination of the trail the next day had shown that she was still a captive of the Indians.

For the time being, however, Jennie knew only that she was, indeed, a captive of the Indians.

When the council ended, the Indians looked across the waters of the Little Sandy River. Then, at a word from the Cherokee chief, he and the other Cherokee, followed by two of the Delawares, and two of the Wyandottes plunged into the muddy water.

Jennie and the Indians who were left stood on the bank of the Little Sandy River and watched them. Their heads and the tops of their shoulders were above water most of the time. Skillfully they dodged the drifts and debris of the flooded river. When they had landed safely on the other side and had disappeared into the forest, Jennie breathed a sigh of relief. For two weeks that had seemed like months she had lived in fear and dread. Now the Cherokee chief was gone.

"God be praised!" she whispered.

The Shawnee chief seemed to consider this separation a blessing, too. The Cherokee had quarreled with him constantly. He had quarreled because the Shawnee had insisted on keeping Jennie as his captive, while the Cherokee had wanted to be rid of her at once. The feeling of ill will between the two chiefs had grown day by day, and this feeling was shared by the other Indians according to their loyalty to one chief or the other. With the departure of the Cherokee chief, the Shawnee was now the acknowledged leader of those who were left: Jennie, one Wyandotte, three Shawnees, and one Delaware. He was happy and thankful for the change in the situation. Since it had come about just as the moon changed, he gave orders for all to worship the new moon according to the Shawnee custom.

A fire was started.

The chief then distributed a mixture of tobacco, dried sumac leaves, and the inner linings of dried bark. He took a portion himself and gave a like portion to each of his followers.

The Indians lined up behind the chief. First in line were the Shawnees, then Jennie. The Wyandotte was last. Jennie felt sure that this order of marching meant that she was now considered a member of the Shawnee tribe, although no words to that effect had been actually spoken.

At a given signal the little band followed the chief around the fire, always moving to the right. Each Indian joined in chanting the words uttered by the chief. The words made

no sense to Jennie, but she did her best to imitate them, not only because she wanted to please the chief, but also because she reverenced any form of worship.

The mixture of tobacco, dried sumac leaves, and dried bark was cast on the fire a bit at a time. It crackled and sparkled and gave off many different colors, and the pungent odor from the burning mixture added a sense of mystery to the rites.

The ceremony lasted for an hour. Then it ended in what seemed to Jennie a kind of silent prayer — a silent prayer so far, at least, as she was concerned. And when the last words of prayer and praise had been said, the little band set off into the forest along the left bank of the Little Sandy River.

"Good weather," said the chief.

"Yes," answered Jennie, who had decided now to cooperate in every way possible. She would make them all think that she was a good Shawnee Indian until the time should come when she could make her escape.

The march was made in a leisurely manner. The Indians hunted and fished and feasted. Fear of being overtaken by the white man had left them entirely. And Jennie, despairing of rescue, turned over and over in her mind ways in which she might escape, if the chance should ever come.

It was good for Jennie that the Indians were in no hurry, for the steady marching exhausted her. Too often she had called upon her reserve strength to carry her through. Too many times she had driven herself to the limit of her endurance. Now that the Cherokee was no longer present, she felt a letdown. She was so tired! Dead tired! She had to force herself to keep up, even when the marching was leisurely.

After crossing the divide that separates the waters of Dry Fork from the waters of Cherokee Creek, Jennie's strength gave way and she became desperately ill — too ill to stand upon her feet.

The Indians sought shelter in a rockhouse nearby and placed Jennie by herself in a small rockhouse on the bank of the stream. Here they left her alone until the next morning.

THE SHAWNEE CHIEF
AS MEDICINE MAN

Before break of day the next morning, the Shawnee chief went to see White Squaw. Jennie could hardly open her eyes, and the chief, seeing that she was seriously ill, now turned medicine man.

"White Squaw must live," he said. "White Squaw not die. White Squaw must live."

He used all the science and art of the Indian medicine he knew in treating the sick woman. He made a pallet of furs and skins for her and put his own blanket over her. After he had made her comfortable, he went into the forest and gathered leaves, herbs, roots, and barks. These he brewed into medicinal teas and tonics for her to take. He cooked gruel for her in his earthenware pots and fed it to her from a wooden spoon. When Jennie lay helpless, he lifted her head gently, and, with his free hand holding tea or gruel to her lips, managed to get her to swallow it. During many long nights he sat patiently by her side as she tossed from one side of the pallet to the other in her delirium. To keep her fever down he bathed her forehead with icy water and kept cold packs on her temples. White Fawn could not have had gentler or more skillful treatment than he gave to Jennie.

To the other Indians he said, "Bring squirrel and partridge for White Squaw. Get wood. Keep White Squaw's fire going."

The Indians did as the chief directed. While hunting in the forest, they killed the small game he requested for Jennie. They kept a supply of wood at hand for a fire by day and night. Otherwise, they paid no attention to Jennie, but left her entirely to the chief's care.

The damp, chilly weather of November was followed by a pleasant, dry December. The nights were clear and cold. The stars and moon shone in all their splendor. The days were warm and there was almost continuous sunshine. This was what Jennie needed. Fine weather, together with nourishing gruels and lean meats and teas and tonics brewed by the Shawnee chief, soon brought her strength back to her.

As soon as she was able to care for herself, the old chief left Jennie to her own devices. No Indian warrior ever did a squaw's work, and Jennie was now expected to take care of herself. Realizing that without the chief's attention she would have died weeks before, Jennie was grateful. She thanked him for all he had done and added, "I will get along all right."

The Indians continued to bring her food. They brought her small game and the choice cuts of larger animals. They brought her skins and furs for blankets and clothing. But they no longer brought wood for her fire. Gathering wood was a squaw's job, and they treated Jennie, now that she was well, exactly as they would have treated her had she been a squaw in one of their native villages.

79

Jennie was pleased that the Indians gave her as much consideration as they did. She knew it was more than most Indian squaws could expect. As for being left to fend for herself, she wanted to be left alone. She wanted to do for herself. And she was thankful that her captors had put her in a rockhouse separated from the one they occupied.

Jennie gathered reeds and coarse grasses from the bank of the creek. She cut willow branches from the trees nearby. From these things, she made a bed for herself and lined it with skins and furs to make it soft and warm.

She made needles from the splinter-like bones found in the leg muscles of the wild turkey. She made sewing awls from the small bones of the deer. She used pieces of sharp flint that the chief gave her for cutting instruments. With

these crude tools she made the skins and furs that were given to her by the Indians into clothing for herself.

The clothes she had been wearing had been torn to tatters. Now she discarded them entirely. The new clothing was not only warmer but it was more suitable for wear in the forest, since it was not easily torn by thorns and briers and brambles.

All her life Jennie had kept herself, her home, and her children tidy and clean. Now that she had the time and the opportunity, she resumed her habits of cleanliness. With the grease of the bear and the lye from the wood ashes she made soap, and this she used in bathing herself and in keeping her living quarters and her cooking utensils clean.

It was good that she was thrown upon her own resources, for this kept her busy. The daylight hours passed quickly. She slept well at night. Instead of brooding over the tragedy that had befallen her, she began to think of the future. She would escape. Somehow or other she would escape and return to her husband.

ON THE MARCH AGAIN

Several months went by in this way, and one beautiful, clear night a new moon again shone in the sky. This, as Jennie knew, would be a sign for worship and rejoicing.

Millions of stars twinkled in the sky, and the Milky Way was a great broad highway across the heavens. The air was crisp. The wind was still.

"What a lovely night for worshiping!" thought Jennie. "Indians worship the new moon. I shall go through their performance, but I shall worship my God."

The Wyandotte started a fire in front of the rockhouse, and the other Indians, shouting and dancing, fed it with sticks and branches. The chief distributed the mixture of tobacco, sumac leaves, and bark to each member of his party. Then he took his place at a distance from the fire and the Indians fell in behind him in the usual ceremonial order. Jennie's place was as usual after the Shawnees. The Indian last in line was the Wyandotte. With great solemnity the line of dancers went around and around the fire, always moving to the right. The fire had burned low. As the ceremonial mixture was cast upon the red embers, a bit at a time, it sparkled and glittered and gave off its peculiar odor. The Indians chanted the moon song, and Jennie joined in the chanting. She had learned the words, although she did not know their meaning. She had learned the rhythmic movements that accompanied the words and danced as though she, too, were worshiping the new moon. The Indians were pleased with her performance.

"White Squaw good Shawnee Indian," said the chief, and all the other Indians agreed.

"I, a Shawnee Indian?" said Jennie to herself. . . . "God forbid!"

When the ceremony was over, the chief said, "Tomorrow we go. White Squaw can march now. Indians not wait longer."

All this time, thought Jennie, they have delayed their march because I was not able to march with them. Why? Why didn't they leave me to die when I lay helpless, or take my life and my scalp and continue on their journey?

To these questions there could be but one answer. In the mind of the chief she was already his daughter. She had taken White Fawn's place. All that remained to make her a Shawnee Indian was the observance of the tribal adoption ceremony.

The thought disturbed her greatly. She was grateful for the protection the chief had given her. He had saved her from death more than once. So long as she remained a captive she needed his protection, but she did not want tribal adoption. She felt that she would die before she would submit to it. Somehow, she determined, she would manage to escape before her captors returned to their villages.

The Indians left the mouth of Cherokee Creek about the first of April. Jennie did not know the exact date. During the days when she had been ill and delirious she had lost all track of time. She did not know the day of the week. She guessed the month only by the position of the sun and by the changes in the weather.

From the rockhouse where they had been sheltered during the winter, the Indians followed the waters of Cherokee Creek to the point where the creek empties into the waters of Big Blaine Creek. They went up Big Blaine Creek to the mouth of Hood Creek. Then they followed Hood Creek for a few hours of leisurely marching, turning right when they reached a small tributary. Soon they came to a rockhouse where they ended their first day's march.

The rockhouse was similar to the one they had occupied on Cherokee Creek, except that it was not quite so open. It extended farther back into the earth and its roof came closer to the ground. Wind seldom blew rain or snow into it. The small stream that flowed less than ten feet away had a rock bottom. Just below the rockhouse the stream fell into a small pool of crystal-clear water. Two hundred feet beyond was a larger waterfall with a larger pool at its base. The top of the rockhouse was covered with vines that hung over its jagged edges, as did the branches of a service tree that was covered with dainty white blossoms.

The sun was going down behind the hills when the party arrived, and its deep red glow crowned the hills with glory. There was a low,

steady roar from the waterfalls, broken by the springtime call of the whippoorwills. Jennie was enchanted and happy when the chief gave orders to make camp.

As on former occasions, the Wyandotte started a fire. Meanwhile three of the Indians went to spear fish in the pool below, and, before dark, they had taken enough for a night of feasting.

The fish were fastened on long sticks and held over the campfire to broil. Jennie relished this meal more than any she had eaten since she had been taken captive.

Late at night, after the feast, everybody lay on the ground around the fire in wheel-like fashion and slept until morning. The Shawnee chief, as always, slept on one side of Jennie and a Shawnee warrior on the other side.

The next morning after the sun was up, a visit was made to a broad plateau above the rockhouse. Here the Indians looked over the grounds, loitered among the trees, and made more conversation with one another than on any occasion since Jennie had been with them. Occasionally they picked up an arrowhead, a broken tomahawk, or a spearhead which lay upon the ground. This made Jennie think that they were paying a visit to a spot where they had camped at some time during a long winter's hunt.

On leaving the plateau, the Indians turned to the right again and, for a short time, it seemed to Jennie that they were traveling in the same general direction from which they had come. Toward noon, they turned to the left. Through a narrow gap they crossed the ridge between the watersheds of Hood Creek and Laurel Creek and descended a small stream to its mouth. Here they found Laurel Creek full of water from melting snow. High cliffs lined the creek's banks on either side, and the swollen waters of the creek were too swift and deep for crossing.

Farther on the Indians found a pine tree that had fallen across the creek. Its butt end rested on the cliff on one side of the creek, and the tip end rested on the cliff on the other side. Here a crossing was made.

From this point they traveled to the flat country where they descended a small stream to Big Mudlick Creek near a point which they referred to as Buffalo Lick, so called because buffalo were often found licking the ground for salt at this particular spot. Here they stopped and made camp. It was good for Jennie that a halt in marching had been called, for she needed rest.

For several days the Indians hunted for buffalo, but each day they returned empty-handed. No buffalo were seen, and the chief finally decided to go on to Little Mudlick Falls, where they were to remain for a long time.

AT LITTLE MUDLICK FALLS

The sun was sinking behind the clouds on the western horizon when the Indians arrived at Little Mudlick Falls. The tops of the hills and ridges in the west were hidden in a narrow streak of dark blue that stretched across the western sky from south to north. The blue blended into streaks of fiery red and orange and gold, broken, here and there, with splotches of black and brown. It was as if a giant, dipping his paintbrush into one great paint bucket after another, had swept his brush across the sky again and again, each time with paint of a different color.

On the plateau the Indians stopped to admire the beauty of the sunset.

"War paint," said the chief, pointing to the western sky.

"War paint! War paint!" replied the other Indians.

"A lovely sunset," said Jennie. "Like war paint, but lovely."

The Indians were happier than Jennie had seen them since they had stood on the bank of the Ohio and shouted "O-hi-yo! O-hi-yo!" They stood above the waterfall and shouted over and over again words which Jennie was sure must mean, "Beautiful falls! Beautiful falls!"

87

From their great rejoicing Jennie strongly suspected that the long march had come to an end; that here they would stay for some time. But this she could only guess, for she was never told anything. If the chief ever spoke of the future in her presence it was always in terms of the adoption ceremony and of what she would do for the Shawnees. He always ended by saying, "White Squaw teach Shawnees to read and write. White Squaw teach Shawnee squaws to sew. White Squaw marry Shawnee warrior."

The thought of such a life made Jennie shudder, but outwardly she gave no sign of her dismay. Inwardly she determined more firmly than ever that, before such things could befall her, she would escape from the Indians or die in the attempt.

The main fall of Mudlick Falls was about thirty feet wide when the creek was full, and about fifteen feet high. At the bottom of this main fall was a beautiful round pool into which the water, pouring over the high cliff, fell with a thunderous roar. There were other falls above the main fall; and below it, for a distance of two hundred feet down the gorge, were many rushing, foaming cataracts and cascades.

The banks of the gorge were covered with rhododendron, mountain laurel, ferns, holly, white dogwood, and redbud, and above them towered poplar, beech, and spruce trees. The cliffs and rocks were covered with moss and with a small vine bearing red berries.

The bark had been stripped from many of the tall trees in the gorge and on the plateau above it. On their bare trunks had been painted in outline pictures of bears, deer, snakes, and other animals, and sometimes pictures of human beings. The paintings were done in a single color, black or red, and the two colors were never mixed. Many of the paintings appeared to be old, while others were evidently very recent.

88

It was to a group of these new paintings that the Indians, after feasting their eyes upon the beautiful falls, directed their steps. They read the message told in pictures as easily as the white man reads the news in his daily paper, but they did not interpret it for Jennie. From what she was able to make of the conversation and of the pictures, the paintings had been done by a band of Indians who were returning from a successful attack upon a white settlement. They had carried off plunder consisting of household articles such as pots and pans. They had driven off the white man's horses and cattle. They had lost some warriors, but they had killed many white settlers and taken their scalps. And they had taken one white woman captive.

A rockhouse was located below the falls. It was more spacious than any the Indians had occupied since Jennie

had been with them. It was large enough to provide sleeping space for hundreds of Indians. It was somewhat the shape of a quarter moon, with a width of twenty-four feet at the center of the arc. Its ceiling was high in front. It faced the gorge and was well protected from the weather. Although the steep bank of the gorge in front of it could be ascended, the best approach to the rockhouse was by means of a narrow ledge that ran alongside the cliff for three or four hundred feet. Sometimes the Indians approached it by climbing down the trees, the tops of which reached the plateau above, where they now stood. It could easily be defended.

This rockhouse, Jennie believed, served as a kind of second home for wandering tribes and roving bands of Indians who might need shelter for short periods of time. She did not believe that there were any permanent Indian settlements in the vast expanse of land that lay between the Ohio and Tennessee rivers.

She did not know why the Shawnee chief had stopped here at this time, but she guessed that the plan had been decided upon earlier. Perhaps the decision had been made at the meeting of the council held on the bank of the Little Sandy River shortly before the Cherokee chief had plunged into its muddy waters and disappeared into the forest on the other side. Whatever the plan, here Jennie was destined to stay for the rest of the spring and the following summer.

COOKING FOR THE INDIANS

The morning after their arrival at Little Mudlick Falls, the chief said to Jennie, "White Squaw cook for Indians, now."

While they were on the march and during their stay at Cherokee Creek, each member of the band had prepared his own food. Jennie had cooked for herself except when she had been too ill to do so, and then the chief had cooked for her. That she might sometime be asked to cook for the Indians had never occurred to her.

She looked about the rockhouse to see if there was anything that could be used for cooking utensils. There was a rusty iron kettle which, no doubt, had been taken from some white woman's kitchen; a few earthenware pots, similar to the pots the chief brewed his medicines in; several shoulder blades of small animals, which could be used for spoons and ladles; and several deer antlers, which could be used for forks. With these things as cooking utensils, she was supposed to cook food for five Indians!

The chief noted the perplexed look on her face. "Chief show White Squaw," he said.

"Thank you," said Jennie.

Cooking for the Indians meant following them on the hunt. It meant skinning the slain animal on the ground where it had been killed and, in the case of large animals such as bears and buffaloes, cutting it into pieces which could be carried to camp. It meant carrying the meat to camp and gathering wood for the fire over which it must be cooked. These, and more too, were Jennie's chores.

The chief was helpful, although he did none of the work. He taught Jennie how to skin an animal. He taught her how to cook as the Indian squaws cooked, for he did not want any of the white woman's way of cooking. After all, he was now teaching White Squaw to become an Indian. In Jennie's first cooking lesson he showed her how to broil small game whole.

"Look!" said the chief. He drove four long forked sticks into the ground about three feet apart so that they formed a square. They stood about thirty inches above the ground. He laid sticks in their forks and cross-laid them with other sticks, making a grill. He started a fire under them and said, "Put meat on sticks. Turn often."

When the meat was broiled to a nice brown, he tried piercing it with a sharp piece of bone. The bone could be inserted quickly and withdrawn easily, so he knew that the meat was sufficiently cooked and took it off the grill. Then he placed it on a ledge of rock to cool.

To stew the meat of small game, he drove two forked sticks into the ground. He hung the iron kettle on a stick that was laid on their forks, filled it with meat and water, and kept a fire going under it.

"Very simple," thought Jennie.

When it came to cooking larger game in Indian style the matter was not so simple. It seemed to Jennie that it required much useless work, but it was not for Jennie to suggest a better method. The chief was the teacher, she

92

was the pupil, and the chief insisted that it be cooked as the Indian squaws cooked it.

In Jennie's first lesson in cooking big game she was taught how to cook the whole carcass of a buffalo at one time. First of all, there was the gathering of wood for the fire.

"White Squaw get wood," the chief said to Jennie early one morning. "Much wood. Buffalo cook a long time."

Jennie went into the hills to gather wood. All morning long she carried branches of trees and dragged pieces of logs to the rockhouse. When she had a big pile of wood, she sat down to rest, thinking, "Surely, this is enough wood to cook a buffalo."

The chief looked it over. "More wood," he said. "White Squaw get more wood."

Again Jennie took up the task. All the afternoon she continued to carry wood to the rockhouse until, by nightfall, she had a pile of wood twice as large as before.

The next morning, before it was daylight, she left with the Indians to hunt buffalo. The animals had been sighted two days before, and the Indians knew just where to find them. It was not long before one had been killed, and then Jennie's task began.

The chief looked at Jennie. "White Squaw skin buffalo," he commanded, placing a flint rock with sharp edges in her hand as a skinning knife. He sat down beside her.

Jennie looked at the large beast. "I have never skinned a buffalo," she thought. "How will I ever be able to do it?"

The chief showed her just where and how to cut the tough hide and how to remove it. Then he showed her how to cut the carcass into chunks of meat that she could carry. It was near midday when the job of skinning the animal and disjointing its carcass had been completed. When it was done, the chief ordered Jennie to carry the meat and the huge hide to the rockhouse.

He showed her how to fold the hide and tie it so that none of its fleshy part was exposed. When she tried to lift it, she found it much too heavy for her to carry. She dragged it over the ground as she had dragged the logs of wood that were too heavy for her to carry.

It was almost sundown when the last piece of meat had been carried to the rockhouse. How many trips had she made? She did not know. She was tired and weary. Nevertheless, the chief said to her, "White Squaw make fire."

Jennie made a fire.

"Put rocks in fire," said the chief.

There was a huge pile of rocks near the spot where he had told her to pile the wood. Until then, Jennie had not known for what purpose they were to be used. She put several large rocks on the fire.

Handing her the shoulder blade of an elk, the chief said, "Make hole."

There was already a hole near the fire, which Jennie now learned was the cooking pit. She scooped out the dirt and leaves that had recently fallen into it. Then the chief ordered her to put the hide in it.

"Put in the hide?" Jennie asked.

"Put in hide," the chief said. "Meat side up!"

Jennie, putting the hairy side down, lined the huge hole with the skin of the animal whose flesh she was to cook. The chief showed her how to stretch the hide and stake it to the ground. Then he said, "Put in meat."

She piled the meat in the hole as directed.

"Get water," said the chief. "Get much water to cook buffalo."

Jennie picked up the leather bags which she used for carrying water and went to the pool at the foot of Mudlick Falls to fill them. It did take "much water" to cook a buffalo, and she made trip after trip until the meat had been covered

94

with water. By this time the stones in the fire were quite hot.

"Put stones in water," said the chief.

"Put stones in water?" Jennie repeated.

"Yes!" commanded the chief.

He found a forked pole for her to use in lifting the huge stones. It was quite a task to lift the hot rocks out of the fire, but Jennie managed somehow and, lifting out one rock after another with the forked pole, dropped each one into the hole that had been filled with meat and water. As the stones cooled, she lifted them from the water and put them back into the fire again. At length, the water was brought to the boiling point.

"Put more wood on fire," commanded the chief. "Keep water boiling."

All night long, Jennie kept wood on the fire and put stones from the fire into the water and back into the fire again. She carried other bags of water which she poured over the meat. Near break of day, the meat showed signs of being tender.

The chief, who had supervised the night-long cooking project, forked a bit of it out with a deer's antler and placed it on a rock to cool. When it had cooled, he tasted it. "Good," he said. "White Squaw good cook."

"God be praised!" Jennie said to herself.

By midmorning, the first lesson in the cooking of big game was over. Tired and weary, Jennie lay down in a corner of the rockhouse and left the Indians to gorge themselves on the food she had cooked.

The cooking of a whole buffalo was by far her hardest and longest job of cooking, but it was never easy to cook for the Indians because they were such big eaters. When they were not hunting, they ate at all hours of the day and night, but no two of them ever seemed to be hungry at the same time.

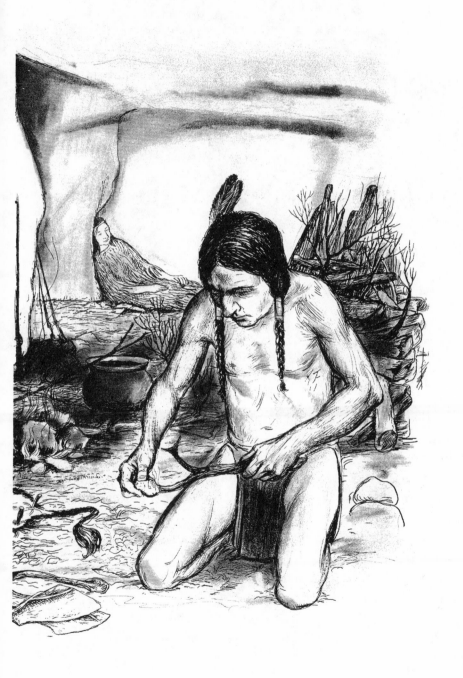

THE BEAR HUNT

One morning the chief said to Jennie, "White Squaw get wood for big fire. Tomorrow Indians hunt bear. Bear in tree."

"Bear in tree," thought Jennie. "That means the bear is still in hibernation. How will the Indians take a bear in hibernation?"

As on the day preceding the buffalo hunt, Jennie gathered wood until she had a huge pile. Early the next morning she left with the Indians to hunt bear.

She followed them through the forest and watched them examine the bark on all hollow trees. Within a short time, the Wyandotte found what they had all been looking for. "Scratched tree!" he called.

The other Indians ran to him. "Scratched tree!" they called to the chief. "Scratched tree! Bear in tree!"

98

When Jennie looked at the tree, she could see that the bark had been torn and scratched wherever the bear had gripped it with its huge claws in climbing up to its winter home.

The scratched tree was a sycamore which stood on the bank of a small stream. It was at least eight feet in diameter at the base but tapered sharply after the first twenty feet in height. Just before the tree began to taper, there was a hole large enough for a bear to crawl through. This, no doubt, was the entrance to the bear's winter home. It had entered the hole during the early part of the winter and had not yet stirred from the long winter nap.

Near the scratched tree was a tall, slender birch which forked at a point just opposite the hole where the bear had entered. The Wyandotte climbed the birch tree. The other Indians handed him a long pole. He placed one end of the pole in the fork of the birch tree and the other in the hole in the sycamore. Then he darted lightly across the pole to the door of the bear's winter home.

He ran another long pole down the hollow of the tree. Down and down it went, but it was too short for his purpose.

With their tomahawks the Indians cut a still longer pole which they handed to him. He ran this one down the hollow tree trunk until it touched the base. There was an angry growl which could be heard even by the Indians standing on the ground.

"Bear in tree!" shouted the Wyandotte, and the other Indians shouted in agreement.

"Get bear out! Get bear out!" they cried.

The Wyandotte punched and poked and punched and poked, but the bear only growled and bit and clawed at the pole.

"Bear not come out," said the Wyandotte.

"Smoke him out," the chief replied.

The Indians built a fire
near the scratched tree.
When it was well started,
they piled the chunks of a
rotten log on it. The rotten
wood burned slowly but
gave off a dense smoke with
an irritating odor.

100

"Smoke bear out," said the chief again.

The Indians fastened the smoking pieces of rotten wood to a pole and handed the pole to the Wyandotte. He dropped the smoldering chunks into the hollow of the tree, and smoke poured out of the hole like smoke from a chimney.

Soon the hunters could hear the sniffing and sneezing of the bear inside the tree. This was followed by a scratching, climbing noise.

"Bear come out!" shouted the Wyandotte, who quickly darted back across the pole to the birch tree and climbed down to the ground.

Each Indian got in position to shoot an arrow into the bear as soon as he should come through the hole in the scratched tree. Before long the bear poked his head through the hole. His eyes were only half open, Jennie thought, and he seemed to be in a stupor.

The Indians stood with drawn bows, their arrows aimed at the bear's head.

"Wait! Wait!" said the chief. "Wait! Wait!"

The smoke continued to pour from the hole through which the bear's head had been thrust. He continued to sniff and sneeze. He put his forepaws outside the tree. He pointed his nose toward the top of the tree and drew his body through the hole.

"Chief shoot!" said the Wyandotte.

The old chief released his arrow. It hit the bear behind the left foreleg and pierced the heart. The arrowhead and a portion of the arrow sank from sight. The other Indians waited breathlessly with drawn bows. The bear clung to the bark of the tree only momentarily. Then its grip relaxed. It dropped to the ground with a heavy thud.

The hunt was over. All of the Indians returned to the rockhouse except the chief, who stayed with Jennie while she skinned the bear and cut its meat into pieces that she could carry.

Jennie had to accompany the Indians on all their hunting trips for two reasons. First, it was her duty to skin the slain animals and carry their carcasses to the rockhouse. Secondly, the Indians were not willing to leave her alone if they could help it. While she had never made an attempt to escape, the chief had set his mind on adopting her as his daughter and he did not intend to let her get away.

On the hunting trips Jennie always kept close behind the chief. She did this because he was more considerate of her than were the other Indians and because, being a medicine man, he was as much on the lookout for herbs and barks as for game. And Jennie wanted to learn the use of plants that grew in the forest.

At Walker's Gap she had often gone with Thomas Wiley into the forest where the ginseng plant grew wild. When the ground around their cabin was too wet to be tilled, one of their chief occupations had been gathering ginseng which they sold at the trading post. They had used a dried, forked hickory stick for digging. They had dug around the long, slender roots of the plant, catching the roots between the prongs of the forked stick and lifting the plant from the soil. Remembering this, her eyes were always looking for the ginseng plant, though, when she saw it she never took it from the forest. Like the Indians, she did not believe in taking anything from nature unless she had immediate need for it.

103

The chief took great pains to teach her about the medicinal plants and their uses. He was pleased that she was interested in plant life and that she learned so readily.

"White Squaw learn!" he said to her.

Jennie enjoyed these trips to the forest. She was gaining knowledge about plant life that she could have gained in no other way. Much of this knowledge would be useful to her all the rest of her life. Besides that, the trips gave her an opportunity to study her surroundings. She studied the hills, the streams, the valleys, and the ridges. She tried to decide in which direction Walker's Gap lay. Much of the time during the first days of her captivity, she had traveled at night. She was not always sure of the direction in which she had traveled. Now, as she looked about her she thought, "Beyond these hills and ridges, somewhere, is Thomas. Over there are my people. Some day I'll escape. Some day I'll go back to them."

Jennie liked hunting. It had been a part of her early training. Her brothers had taught her how to shoot a rifle. At the age of twelve years she could lay the long barrel of her brother's rifle in the fork of a stick which had been stuck upright in the ground and "bark" a squirrel at a distance of one hundred paces. This meant hitting the branch on which a squirrel was sitting and killing it from the impact alone, without the bullet's touching its body. Often she had provided the meat for her father's table, and later her husband's table, in this manner. Once, after she was married, she had shot a bear. The bear had torn down the pigsty and had taken their only pig, which was being fattened for pork. Jennie, hearing the squealing of the pig, had run

104

to the door to see what was the matter. The bear had caught the pig in its forepaws and, walking upright, was carrying it off into the forest. How the pig had squealed! But the squealing had only made the bear hug its prey tighter. She had grabbed the rifle from the rack above the fireboard, run out into the yard, and stuck the forked stick in the ground. Placing the barrel of the rifle in the fork, she had aimed at a spot between the bear's shoulders. When she pulled the trigger, the bear had hit the ground and the frightened pig had run back to the sty. Yes, Jennie Wiley knew how to shoot a rifle!

How she wished the Indians would let her use one of the rifles which they themselves seldom used in hunting. But the Indians, of course, had no intention of taking a chance on what she might do with a rifle in her hands. And so she had to content herself with trapping and snaring, which seemed to her the hard way to hunt.

She was not entirely a beginner in trapping and snaring small game, either. She had often helped Thomas Wiley run his traps. She knew how to make a deadfall, and she had been bold enough to say so to the chief, who nearly always insisted upon showing her how a thing was to be done.

"Let me make a deadfall," she said to him on one occasion when they had located the den of an opossum.

"Make deadfall," he answered.

She found a small straight hickory about an inch in diameter. This she cut into three lengths; one of eighteen inches, one of twelve, and one of nine inches. She cut notches in the sticks so that they would hold together when arranged in the shape of a figure 4. She placed one end of a large rock upon the upright piece, letting the other end rest on the ground behind the trap. Then she tied a piece of meat on the free end of the horizontal piece of the deadfall.

The chief viewed her handiwork with admiration. "Deadfall catch opossum," he said.

Jennie's trap did catch opossum, and other traps that she made caught mink, muskrat, coon, and other small animals. She dug deep round holes in paths where rabbits ran, placed light sticks over them, and then covered the sticks with leaves. Rabbits fell into the holes and were taken alive.

Wild turkey, grouse, and quail were caught in pens. A pen was made from sticks or small poles notched and fitted over each other in much the same way that the walls of a cabin are put together except that, for the pen, each layer of sticks or poles was shorter than the layer just before it. This brought the pen to a point at the top. A heavy pole was placed over the top and the ends tied to the bottom pieces of the pen on two sides. Thus, there was no danger of the wind blowing the pen to pieces.

Jennie usually built the pen on the gentle slope of a hill near the roosting place of the birds she hoped to catch. She built it over a narrow trench that was just wide enough for one bird to enter at a time. The portion of the trench nearest the wall inside the pen was covered over with bark. Wild seeds and grains which Jennie gathered solely for this purpose were strewn along the trench. The unsuspecting birds followed the line of grains and seeds into the pen. Once inside the pen, they tried to get out not by the same way they had entered, but by flying against its walls. They were trapped.

The chief looked at the first pen Jennie built for birds and nodded his head approvingly. "White Squaw's snare catch turkey," he said.

White Squaw's snare did catch turkey. It caught grouse and quail as well. Much of the roast fowl enjoyed by the Indians was trapped in this manner.

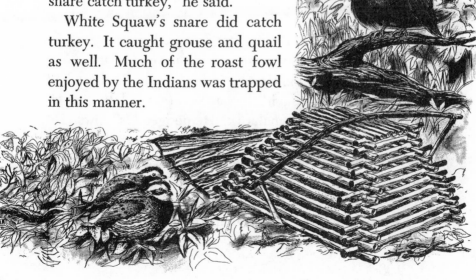

INDIAN VISITORS

The Indian always wanted to take the enemy unaware, but he never wanted to surprise his neighbor or his tribe with an unexpected visit. When he was within signaling distance, he announced that he was coming. He continued to make announcements until his approach was acknowledged. He then told his business, where he had been, what he had accomplished, and what his destination was. The purpose of this announcement was to prepare his host for his reception. He expected to be entertained in the best manner possible.

When he finally arrived, after this exchange of signals, he went through a performance that showed in pantomime the exploits he had announced in his signals. If there had been a battle, he refought the battle. He struck the imaginary enemy with his tomahawk. He dodged his blows. He scalped his victim. In acting out these episodes, the Indian was likely to exaggerate, for putting on a good show was as important as revealing his accomplishments. He was expected to be an accomplished actor.

One morning the chief, watching from the plateau, called to Jennie, "Signals! Signals!"

108

Jennie came to the plateau where the chief stood and looked in the direction in which he was pointing. There to the west three small clouds of smoke, one above the other, rose lazily into the sky. They were followed by another and then by two more.

"Delaware Indians," said the chief.

An hour later the firing of guns near the mouth of Little Mudlick Creek was heard. Three shots rang out. There was a pause and then a fourth shot was heard, soon followed by two others.

The chief gathered his little band on the plateau above the rockhouse. Shots were fired in reply. There was an exchange of whoops and shrieks. From the conversation of the Indians about her, whose speech Jennie was by now beginning to understand, she learned that the visitors were a mongrel band of Indians composed mostly of Delawares. They were twenty-one in number. They were returning from a scouting expedition which had been uneventful. No white men had been sighted.

When this mongrel band arrived on the plateau, Jennie saw that the leader was a Delaware warrior. He was tall, straight, and slender. He went through the pantomime according to custom, but since there were no long or unusual events to portray, the show was soon over.

The chief called a meeting of the council. Jennie was not permitted to attend, but she observed that the meeting was friendly, and that the Indians were congenial. She believed that they discussed things which interested all of them, including her own fate.

When the council meeting was over, the visitors turned their attention to White Squaw, and the leader of the newcomers said to her, "Cook meat. Hurry. Indians hungry."

There was something in the tone of his voice and in his manner which reminded her of the fierce and brutal

109

Cherokee. Not wishing to provoke his anger, she was thankful for the experience she had had in cooking for the Shawnee chief and his followers. Though she had been cooking for them for less than a month, she had learned a lot about the eating habits of the Indians. She knew how they wanted their meat cooked and about how much it took to satisfy them.

Fortunately the Shawnee chief had killed a deer that morning. Jennie had spent the whole day dressing it, and it was now ready to go on the grill and into the kettle. There was also the hindquarter of a bear that had not yet been cooked. All together there was just about enough to feed the Indians.

The fires were already going. Jennie filled the iron kettle with the pieces of meat that were easiest to boil and hung it over the fire. Then she cut the pieces that were suitable for broiling into thin strips and placed them on the grill. She kept the fires going. She turned the broiled pieces with the forked antlers and every so often she stirred the boiling meat with the bone ladle to make sure it did not catch on the bottom of the kettle.

When the meat in the kettle was tender, she forked it from the kettle and placed it upon a rock which she had covered with a deer hide. As the broiled pieces were ready, she took them off the grill and set them beside the rest. She refilled the kettle, and placed other pieces of meat on the grill to broil. This process she repeated over and over again until all of the meat had been cooked.

The Indians enjoyed the feast immensely, but they gave her no thanks for it. Each time that they grabbed what she had placed on the rock for them, it was with the command to cook more. After feasting until late at night, they lay down upon the ground and slept until morning. Before daylight they were again on their way.

110

This band of Indians was followed within a week by another band of seven. When they approached the mouth of Little Mudlick Creek, they gave the customary signal. The chief assembled his party on the plateau above to receive them and to watch their pantomime. As with the previous band, nothing unusual had occurred, so their pantomime, too, was short and not very dramatic. But this band of Indians remained for several days, and during that time Jennie cooked great quantities of food for them.

Shortly after their departure, still another band led by a Delaware chief arrived. There was the same kind of signaling from the mouth of Little Mudlick Creek and the same kind of reception, but the pantomime acted on arrival by the Delaware was of a fiercer nature. He and his band had been upon the warpath. He had lost some warriors and had killed some white settlers. Their scalps dangled from the belts of his warriors. The chief's performance showed that they had surprised the white men at work in a field and had fired upon them from ambush; that the white men had run for their guns; that fighting had ensued; and that the victims had been scalped. With what exaggeration he portrayed the incident!

Later on, after the council meeting, each of the newcomers treated Jennie as if she were his property, and ordered her about at will. The Shawnee chief from whom Jennie, until now, had received signs of kindness and of protection did nothing about it. Jennie realized more than ever before that, as a captive, she must obey any member of any band until finally released to her captor.

HUNDREDS OF FISH

A day came that was as lovely as a day in June, and yet Jennie knew by the signs about her that even April was not yet gone. The buds on the oak trees, just bursting open, cast a veil of grayish green over the forest. The first tiny leaves of the white ash, the maple, and the poplar were beginning to show. The white dogwoods were in bloom, and redbuds, too. The last faded blossoms of the service tree still clung to the tip ends of the trees that dotted the forest here and there. Patches of violets clustered about the bases of the giant sycamores, and clumps of bloodroot nestled at the foot of the sugar maples. Spring had transformed the hills overlooking Little Mudlick Falls into beauty.

The Indians sat in the warm springtime sun and whittled on their bows and arrows, chipped their flints, or turned their attention to other small tools for hunting and fishing.

Jennie saw the chief lay aside the unfinished tomahawk on which he was working. He looked at the hills about him. He pushed his arms above his head, brought them down to the height of his shoulders, and pushed them up again. He shrugged his shoulders once or twice. Then he said to her, "Catch fish."

What he had said sounded like an invitation, but Jennie knew he did not give invitations. He gave commands.

"Very well," she replied. "Let's catch fish."

112

The chief arose from his sitting position. Without taking a spear, bow and arrows, or anything else that an Indian uses in fishing, he walked down the gorge. Jennie followed in his footsteps.

A short distance below the gorge there was a narrow, deep stretch of water, perhaps fifty feet long. It was a kind of pocket in the bend of the creek. At the mouth of it logs had been placed in the creek to form a V-shaped barricade.

At one end the logs rested on the bank and at the other end they came together near the center of the creek in the form of a huge V. Placed one on top of another, until the barricade reached high-water level, the top logs did not touch at the point of the V. The barricade had been staked in place, and brush, stones, and rocks had been piled behind it. Water-soaked and covered with moss and green scum, it seemed to Jennie that the barricade must have been there for years and years. Through the narrow opening at the top of the barricade water flowed spout-like, then spread out again over the bottom of the stream from bank to bank. Jennie had never seen anything like it and wondered how it came to be there.

"Cherokee Indians make this," said the chief. "Cherokee Indians catch fish here."

The chief dragged from the bushes, where it had been lying for at least a season, a net made of bark and leather. It was weather-beaten and the bark was brittle in places, but it was still whole. He looked it over. "Good," he said. "Hold fish."

Jennie helped him fasten it to the logs that were just below the place where the water spouted from the pool.

"Get bushes," he said to her. "Big branches."

Jennie found two hawthorn bushes that had large branches. Although they were thorny, she cut them with the stone hatchet

113

which she carried in the leather belt around her waist and took them to the chief.

He took one and told her to keep the other. Then he waved her over to the other side of the pool.

Jennie waded across the upper end of the pool.

"Hit water," the chief said to her. "Make noise."

With her hawthorn branch, Jennie struck the water on one side of the pool and the chief with his branch struck it on

the other side. Their branches almost met in the center of the pool. Time after time they struck the water, making as much noise as they could.

Jennie could see the frightened fish dart across the pool from one side to the other and then follow the logs downstream to the point of the V. Here they were carried over the barricade and into the net, one after another.

114

For several minutes Jennie and the chief kept up the terrific beating of the water. It was exciting to see the fish dart into the net, but soon the chief said, "Much fish. Pull up net."

They untied the net and dragged it out of the water and up the bank. It was filled with flopping fish. The old chief emptied them out upon the ground, picked out the fish he did not want to keep, and tossed them back into the water. Then he and Jennie gathered up the rest and put them in a kettle which Jennie had brought along.

"Good fishing," he said to Jennie.

"Yes, it is," she replied.

There were never any leisure moments for Jennie. She kept busy even when she was not required to by the Indians. But during the next several days, when she could spare a few moments from other things, she made a new net of bark and leather. She made a fish basket, also. With this she could do much fishing by herself.

The fish basket was about six feet long and two feet in diameter. It was made from hoops and long straight sticks and bark and leather. One end of it was closed. At the other end were three funnels of leather, one inserted into another. They could be removed at will. The funnel nearest the outside of the basket was eighteen inches long, the one in the middle was twelve inches, and the one inside was nine. The opening in the small end of each funnel was just big enough for a good sized fish to swim through.

Jennie carried the basket to the pool. She tied one end of a long piece of leather to it and tied the other end to a bush on the bank near the pool. She put several pieces of stale meat inside the basket, tied a stone to it for a sinker, and tossed it into the water.

The next morning the chief went with her to the pool. She pulled the basket to the bank and tried to lift it out of

115

the water. It was too heavy. The chief gave her a helping
hand. It was so full of fish that it was all they could do,
both together, to lift the basket from the water. The old
chief's eyes sparkled.

"Basket catch fish," he said.

Jennie removed the funnels and turned the flopping,
floundering fish onto the ground.

"Good fishing," the chief remarked. "Much fish."

Jennie always kept the fish basket baited. She saved
bones and bits of meat that she did not care to cook and
put them into the basket. At any time she wanted fish, all
she had to do was raise the basket.

The chief taught her how to spear fish. He made a spear
with a barbed point for her and taught her how to use it.

He taught her how to shoot fish with bow and arrow. Often they fished together.

Sometimes Jennie sat on the top log of the barricade on one side of the pool and the chief sat on the top log on the other side. They sat and watched and waited. When a fish swam alongside the logs, they speared it.

Sometimes the chief let her fish by herself, although she knew that she was probably being watched from the bushes by someone. She sat on the top log of the barricade in the warm sun and fished and daydreamed. She made plans and laid schemes for making her escape.

Under the circumstances, nothing could be fun for Jennie, but fishing provided a kind of diversion that she needed.

LEAD INTO BULLETS

It was another glorious spring morning, almost the most beautiful one that Jennie had seen since her arrival at Little Mudlick Falls. Swallows were building their nests of moss and mud in crevices in the ceiling of the rockhouse. Young squirrels were chasing each other through the limbs of the trees outside. What a fine day just to look at the world and enjoy its beauty! But no such pleasure was in store for Jennie.

"White Squaw get wood," the chief told her. "Wood melt lead."

"Wood melt lead," Jennie repeated to herself. "What does he mean?"

She went into the hills to gather wood. She had to go far, since most of the wood in the gorge and on the plateau had already been gathered.

Jennie could do very little chopping because she had only a stone ax with which to chop. That meant that she must find pieces of wood, parts of rotten logs, branches that the wind had blown off the trees, and small dead trees. These she could uproot with her hands and break in pieces

118

by placing one end on a nearby log and jumping on the middle part.

"Wood melt lead," she thought. "What kind of wood?"

She decided that she would need wood that would burn for a long time, and make a hot fire while it burned. Therefore, she hunted for the rotten logs of black pine trees. These would have pine knots rich in resin and yet long burning. She found them at the top of the hills. She chopped them in pieces as well as she could with her stone ax and carried the rich pine knots to the plateau above the rockhouse. She tore bark from dry logs that were too heavy to carry. She picked up sticks and branches. All day long she gathered wood.

The old chief loitered in the woods nearby to keep an eye on her. The other Indians lolled in the sun and watched the pile of wood grow with each additional load she carried to it.

At night the chief said to her, "More wood to melt lead. Get more wood tomorrow."

All the next day she carried wood. Each time she went for a new load she had to go a greater distance. At the end of the day her shoulders were sore, her hands blistered. There were splinters in her fingers and one fingernail was missing.

That night the chief repeated his statement of the night before: "More wood to melt lead. White Squaw get more wood."

She did not sleep that night. Her muscles were tired. Her back hurt. Her legs ached. As she turned and tossed and tried to find a comfortable position, she thought of trying to make her escape. But to escape now would be impossible, she knew. She must wait until she could travel some hours at least before the Indians would miss her. Even then, success would not be certain.

119

The next day she repeated the work of the two preceding days. Over and over again she said to herself, "Jennie Wiley. Jennie Wiley. You must escape. You must escape!"

The third night the chief said, "Plenty wood. Tomorrow White Squaw get lead."

The next morning, before the sun had risen, the Indians were up, eager to go to the lead mine. Jennie was eager to go, too. If there was a lead mine near Little Mudlick Falls, she wanted to know about it. Some day she would lead Thomas Wiley and others of her people to it.

Armed with their stone axes, their digging tools, and leather bags in which to carry the lead ore, the Indians and Jennie set out for the mine. When they had been traveling for thirty or forty minutes, the chief said to Jennie, "White Squaw stay. Indians get lead."

Jennie watched the Indians disappear into the forest. Each went in a different direction. When they returned a short time later with the ore, each came from a different direction. Jennie knew their crafty ways. She knew that their purpose was to mystify her — to keep secret from her the location of the mine.

The big pieces of rock containing bits of lead were poured out upon the ground for Jennie to carry. She filled her leather bag and began her task. All day long she carried the heavy ore to the plateau above the rockhouse, returning each time to fill her bag again. Still the pile for her to carry mounted. The Indians could dig out the ore and put rocks on the pile faster than she could carry them away. It took her two days to transport the ore which they dug in one day.

On the second day following the trip to the mine, the smelting process was begun. The chief, as usual, stood near to supervise the work.

"White Squaw dig," he said.

He showed her where to dig a trench on the side of the plateau that sloped gently toward the gorge. The trench was about ten feet long, about six inches wide, and not more than five inches deep. At the lower end of the trench she dug a shallow hole.

A fire was built over the upper end of the trench and, when it was roaring, the chief told Jennie to put the rocks in it. After she had put some of the ore in the fire, he ordered her to pile more wood on top of the ore.

"Big fire," he said.

Jennie piled on more wood. Shortly, she noticed a white stream of molten lead trickling slowly down the trench to the shallow hole at the bottom, where it cooled and hardened. After the lead was melted from the ore, she lifted the rocks from the fire with the forked stick that she used when she cooked buffalo. Then she put other pieces of ore into the fire, and piled more wood on top of them.

This process she kept up all day long. By nightfall, there was a mass of lead half the size of a gallon bucket. The Indians then remelted the pure lead and moulded it into bullets.

This was Jennie's first experience in the art of smelting, and it was an experience she was to repeat at least once each month during the rest of her captivity. But try as hard as she might, she was never able to see the lead mine. Even when she hunted with the Indians and knew she was near its location, she could discover no sign of it. The Indians always concealed its entrance, after they had worked in it, as carefully as they concealed the ashes of an overnight campfire.

The Indians had killed a large deer, and Jennie had skinned the beautiful animal. She had cut it up and carried every piece of it to the rockhouse, where she was preparing to cook it. The chief sat on a stone nearby, watching her prepare the forequarters.

"Not cook bones," he said. "Take meat off."

Jennie wondered why the meat was to be taken from the bones, but as usual she did as the chief directed and asked no questions.

After she had removed the meat from the bones, the chief said, "Scrape bones."

She scraped the two shoulderblades until they glistened in the sun. The chief took them in his hands and looked them over. He threw one onto the pile of bones and bits of meat that Jennie had saved for the fish basket, and kept the other.

He cut a tall, straight hickory about two inches in diameter and chopped a five-foot piece off the butt end of it. Jennie watched him remove the bark from the stick and make a deep split down the center of one end. Then inside the split, she saw him cut notches on either side three inches from the end. Into these notches he fitted the neck end of the shoulder blade. He tried to pull the split sides of the stick together above the shoulder blade, but they did not close perfectly. He removed the bone, cut the notches deeper, and inserted the bone again. This time the pieces closed firmly. He wrapped and tied the split

122

ends with rawhide. He wrapped and tied them as firmly as he tied his tomahawk or his stone ax onto its handle. Then he handed it to Jennie. The crude tool looked like a hoe, and she wondered what she was to do with it.

The chief took down a leather bag filled with Indian maize that had hung suspended from the ceiling of the rockhouse and handed it to her. Then he pointed to the leaves on the oak trees which were about the size of a mouse's ear.

"Leaves show time for planting," he said. "Plant maize. Chief show White Squaw how."

Followed by Jennie, he walked down the side of the gorge to the narrow bottom land at the base of the plateau.

During the winter and the early spring months, the bottom land had been covered with backwater many times. Mud and silt and loam had been left upon it together with debris of various kinds. The warm spring sun had dried it and cracked it in many places, but Jennie could see that it was fertile ground.

"Clean off and plant maize," the chief said to her.

Jennie began the difficult task of clearing off the debris from the place where she was to plant the maize. The chief sat on a log nearby and watched her. When all of the debris had been cleared away, she marked off straight rows about three feet apart. Then at intervals in the rows she dug shallow holes with her hoe, dropped two kernels of corn in each hole, as she had done when she had helped Thomas Wiley plant his corn, and covered them over with earth and sand.

In about ten days, tiny shoots began to break through the soil. Jennie noticed them at once, but so did the squirrels that lived in the trees nearby. Late in the afternoon and early each morning, they could be seen digging down beside the slender shoots to the grain at their base.

Jennie's **dog** Tige had been a great help to her in hunting and trapping small game. Now she took him with her to the cornfield to chase the squirrels away from her corn. Since squirrels did not hunt food during the hot middle part of the day, Jennie and Tige stayed from break of day until midmorning, returning again at midafternoon and remaining until dark. Sometimes the Indians went with her to shoot squirrels for food, but they never killed more than were needed for that purpose.

Jennie kept watch over the corn until the growing plants had consumed the grain at their roots. Then her work took on a different nature. The plants grew rapidly in the fertile soil, but so did the weeds. She pulled the weeds with her hands and cultivated the soil about the plants with her hoe. She had never worked harder on Thomas Wiley's farm than she worked in the Indians' field of maize, but her knowledge of gardening stood her in good stead and she liked to see things grow under her care. Frequent light summer rains and constant cultivation made the garden plot prosper. In about three months the maize began to silk out and tassel.

124

When the silky tassels on the green ears began to turn brown, the chief went with Jennie each day to the cornfield. They walked between the rows of corn from one end of the field to the other. The chief broke open the husk at the tip of the ear on all the ears where the tassels were dry. He pinched the tender grains with the tips of his fingers, but none were picked until there were enough ripe ears for a feast. Then the Indian Corn Dance was held.

After the Corn Dance, Jennie went to the cornfield to gather corn. She broke the ears off the stalks and carried armloads of them to the rockhouse. Then, in the hot, glowing embers of the fire, she roasted the ears of corn in their husks. As soon as the husks were brown and parched she stripped them off and placed the sweet, juicy ears where the Indians could get them.

The new corn, fresh from the field, was so good that each of the five Indians ate more than enough corn for all of them together. Even Jennie herself, tasting the corn, knew that it was good and that she had earned the praise of the chief when he said, "White Squaw good cook."

So long as there was corn the Indians did little hunting or fishing. They ate only corn roasted in the husk or boiled in the iron kettle.

In the fall Jennie gathered the ears of corn that had been left on the stalks until they were dry and good for seed. She carried the ears to the rockhouse where she stripped them and placed them in leather bags. These she hung from the ceiling where, out of reach of mice or squirrels, they would be ready for next year's planting.

125

BUFFALO ROBES
AND DEERSKIN CLOTHES

It was the custom of the Indians to tan the hides
and furs of animals killed during the spring and summer
just as carefully as those of animals killed during the winter.
Tanning them and making them into clothing and other
useful articles fell, for the most part, to the lot of the Indian
squaws. Thus it became Jennie's duty, as the only woman
in the group, to work with the hides and furs of animals
which had been killed for meat. Her first big job after going
to Mudlick Falls was the tanning of a buffalo hide which
she was later to use as a blanket.

"Chief show how," the chief said, as usual, when she
started on the task.

"Stretch hide on ground," he said, pointing to the huge
hide. "Stretch."

Jennie spread the huge hide upon the ground with the
hairy side down. She staked one side of it to the ground

126

with sharp sticks. She had to stake it firmly enough so that it would not give when she took hold of the opposite side and pulled with all her might.

"Pull," the chief kept saying. "Pull!"

Jennie pulled and pulled. When she had stretched the hide as much as she could, she staked the further side of it to the ground. Then she stretched the hide at the two ends and staked them.

"Take off fat," said the chief, handing her a piece of flint rock with sharp edges, to use as a scraper. "Take off fat!"

Jennie took the scraper and scraped off the fat. She scraped and scraped until the hide was clean and no piece of fat was left anywhere.

Earlier, when she had prepared the meat for cooking, she had made, under the direction of the chief, a mixture of brains, bone marrow, and liver. She had had to mix it as thoroughly as she could, squeezing it in her hands and fingers until it was a gluey substance, but at the time she made it she had not known for what purpose the mixture was to be used.

Now the chief set the mixture before her and pointing to it, said, "Rub. Rub hide."

She rubbed the mixture into the hide with her hands. She rubbed and rubbed. Then she rolled it with a short round pole. Back and forth, from side to side and from end to end, she rolled it. This was to make the hide soft and pliable.

When this had been done, the chief told her to put the hide into a nearby pit which had been lined with skins so that it would hold water. Jennie pulled up the stakes, dragged the hide to the pit, and threw it in.

"Get bark from chestnut oak," the chief directed.

Jennie took her stone ax and went with the chief to a large chestnut oak tree that stood at the top of a hill. Al-

127

though the sap had risen and the bark did not stick tightly to the tree, it was still difficult to chop through the thick bark and tear it loose from the tree. After a few hours of hard work, she had enough bark for her purpose and carried it to the pit. Here she chopped and pounded it to small pieces and covered the hide with it. Then she covered the hide with water.

The hide was left in the solution of water and chestnut oak bark for several days. When it could be seen that the hide had turned the color of the bark, it was taken out of the solution and again rubbed with the mixture of brains, bone marrow, and liver. This was the last step, and after it had been left in the sun to dry, it was ready to be used as a blanket.

The skin of the deer was frequently tanned for leather. The fresh skin was put in a pit, hairy side up, and covered with a thin layer of ashes. The ashes were then sprinkled with water and kept moist until the hair slipped from the skin, a process which usually took several days. When all the hair had been removed, the skin was put into the pit again and soaked in the chestnut oak bark solution until, like the buffalo hide, it turned the color of the bark. It was taken from the solution and rubbed with the same mixture of brains, bone marrow, and liver. After it had dried, it was ready for all the purposes for which the Indians used leather.

The furs and skins of smaller animals were stretched upon pieces of bark or tacked to trees. The fat was removed

128

with the scraper and the fleshy side was greased and rubbed soft. After that the grease was removed with soap and water, and the skins were thoroughly dried.

Jennie did all of this work under the supervision of the chief, who watched her but never offered to help her. Every skin had to be preserved in this manner. After each hunt the chief made a count to see that none was missing.

Jennie was allowed to use all of the skins and furs she wanted or needed for her own clothing, but she was not required to make anything for the Indians except blankets and robes. This may have been because summer was coming on and the Indians wore little clothing in summer.

Jennie enjoyed making leather garments for herself. She liked to sew, and sewing, like fishing, was a kind of diversion for her. She made long leather skirts with fringed edges. She made short leather jackets and trimmed the edges with furs. She cut them according to the pattern she had used for the linsey-woolsey materials she had once made into dresses. For her feet, the chief taught her how to make moccasins after the Shawnee fashion.

Jennie always went fully dressed, though the Indians could not understand why she wrapped herself in leather on a hot summer day. Back in their villages the squaws wore only short skirts with nothing above the waist. For themselves, they wore in hot weather only the breachclout drawn between the legs and tied to a belt around the waist. The Indian thought himself well dressed when his breachclout was in place and his body had been coated with bear's grease. But although the Indians wondered about Jennie and were amazed that she was always fully dressed, they let her have her own way in the matter of her personal clothing.

RETURN OF THE CHEROKEE

The bud, the leaf and flower, the fruit, and the harvest had come and gone in their seasons. Now the dark green leaves of the black gum trees had turned to the deep red color of wine. The broad leaves of the poplar were golden yellow; those of the sugar maple bright crimson. The slender leaves of the sourwood had turned to dark, dark purple, and the leaves of the oak were rusty brown. The rabbit had left its summer home in the lowlands for a warmer home in the grassy tufts on the south hillside. Yes, the spring, the summer, and the first month of fall had come and gone.

Nobody, not even Jennie, had observed these seasonal changes more closely than had the Shawnee chief. Nobody was more concerned than he about them. "Two moons till winter," he said to Jennie. "Cherokee not come back."

Jennie could see the look of disappointment on his face. During the summer, as each of the roving bands of Indians had arrived for a visit, the chief, she remembered, had been happy. He had been eager to receive them. But each time, after the council meeting, he had seemed disappointed. Now she thought she understood the reason. He had been expecting Indians who would take over his responsibility at the rockhouse, whatever that responsibility might be, and those Indians had never come.

130

"Chief go back to tribe," he continued. "Make White Squaw Indian." Jennie knew these remarks meant that he wanted to get home to the Shawnee village where she could be adopted by the tribe.

During the spring, the summer, and the fall, Jennie had worked hard every minute of the daylight hours and sometimes until far into the night. She had hunted and fished, gathered wood, tanned hides, and dressed furs. She had made blankets and robes for the Indians and clothing for herself. She had sometimes cooked for as many as thirty Indians at a time. She had planted, cultivated, and harvested a crop of maize. She had carried great piles of lead ore and smelted the ore for a little bit of lead. During all this time, the Indians had never turned a hand to help her. She had slaved for them. She had been considerate of the visitors, partly because she had little choice, but partly, too, because she hoped that sometime some one of them might speak about the white settlers. But a white person had never been mentioned except when Indian visitors sometimes spoke of settlers who had been killed or taken captive.

"In two months winter will come," she said to herself. "The chief wants me adopted by his tribe. If I don't escape, one of two things will happen. The chief and his warriors may spend the winter in the rockhouse. Then they will hunt for furs, and more animals will be killed and more skins and furs will have to be tanned. There will be visits from other roving bands of Indians, and that will mean more cooking for me to do. How can I stand another six months of such labor and servitude? But if, on the other hand, Indians come to take over the chief's responsibility here, he will return to the Shawnee villages north of the Ohio. Then I shall be adopted by the tribe. If that happens, I shall become a slave forever." For Jennie knew that if she were married to one of the chief's warriors, not only would her

131

Indian husband treat her as a squaw, but the other squaws of the tribe would treat her as a slave. The humiliations and the hard physical drudgery they would put upon her would be more than she could endure. There was only one thing for her to do. She must escape.

There had been occasions when it had seemed to her that the time had come for her to make her escape, but each time something seemed to say to her, "Not yet." And so she had waited.

The days went by. The sun rose a little later each morning and set a little earlier each evening. Each day the crisp fall air became colder. And each day Jennie, troubled by the thought of approaching winter, felt that she must not put off her attempt to escape much longer.

One day the chief and his warriors killed a bear and a deer. Jennie skinned them, as usual, and carried the hides and meat to the rockhouse. She cooked the meat at night, and the Indians spent the next day in feasting. In the evening, as they were loitering about a small fire near the center of the rockhouse, a long, weird call came up the narrow valley from the mouth of Big Mudlick Creek. It came from farther away than any call had come before, and it almost seemed to bounce from hill to hill.

Jennie's blood ran cold. She had heard that voice before. It was the voice of the Cherokee chief.

Jennie felt sure, from the changing expressions on the face of the Shawnee chief and from his tone of voice when he spoke to his followers, that this was an anxious moment. She knew that the Shawnee had been looking forward to the return of the Cherokee, even though she knew, too, that he feared the Cherokee and distrusted him.

The Shawnee led his little band, including Jennie, to the plateau above the rockhouse where he gave the answering call. There was the usual exchange of signals. Then the

132

Shawnee chief said to Jennie, "Cherokee angry. Fight white settlers. Lose warriors. Take white captive."

Jennie's heart almost stopped beating. "Cherokee chief angry," she said to herself. "He has lost warriors. He has taken a white captive. Nothing good can come from our meeting."

She stood on top of the plateau with the Shawnee chief and his warriors and waited — waited for the Cherokee chief who had killed her children and her brother. She watched him and his followers wend their way through the forest. Up the hill to the top of the plateau they came.

The Cherokee chief led the line of march as he had done for the nine days she had marched behind him. His strides were long, fast, and even. He carried himself erect. His face was smeared with war paint, and he was dressed in his war regalia, with red shirt, buckskin leggings, and beaded moccasins. His huge, silver rings dangled from his ears, and along with his knife and tomahawk, green scalps hung from his belt. Following him there seemed to be an endless chain of Indians. Jennie recognized some of them as the Indians who had been with him when she was taken captive. On they came, twenty-three in number. Next to the last Indian in line was a young white man whose hands were tied behind him.

Yes, the Cherokee chief, the terror of the forest, had returned.

TORTURE

The Indians were in a restless, noisy mood when they reached the top of the plateau. They were excited and angry. Jennie guessed from what the Shawnee chief had said that, although they had succeeded in taking a captive, they had fought an unsuccessful battle with white settlers. There was no exchange of friendly greetings as there had been when other bands of Indians had arrived for a visit. Instead, the Cherokee stamped about with a scowl on his face. He paced back and forth before the Shawnee chief and before his band of followers like a caged lion. He looked at the Shawnee chief and muttered something which Jennie did not understand. The Shawnee chief made no reply.

When the Cherokee chief looked at Jennie, it was with contempt and scorn, but he said nothing to her, nor was he, evidently, talking about her. His mind was on the victim he had recently captured.

"It is not my turn yet," thought Jennie, but her heart sank within her as she saw the Indians, at the order of the Cherokee, forming in two lines. That must mean that the white

135

prisoner was to run the gantlet. The Indians in each of the two lines were far enough apart so that each Indian could swing his club with all his might without touching the Indian on either side of him. The lines themselves were close enough together so that there was no place between the two lines where the runner could escape from any of the blows.

The Shawnee chief and his followers had cut branches from a hawthorn tree and had taken their places in the lines. They, like the other Indians, seemed ready to enjoy a share in the brutal beating of the white man. Jennie's fear for her own treatment was doubled by seeing the Shawnee chief himself brandishing his hawthorn stick and enjoying the excitement.

Although she was never permitted to get close to him, Jennie guessed that the white man was a youth of about twenty years. He was of medium height and muscular build. His body bore evidence of the shameful punishment he had already taken. His face was bruised and there were black-and-blue marks around his eyes. His arms and back had been cut by the lashes he had received. These marks, together with wounds on his legs and great red welts on his body, showed how brutally he had been treated.

The youth's hands had been tied behind him. To them was attached a strip of rawhide about six feet in length which served as a leash. The Cherokee chief, the same warrior who had taken the life of Batt Sellards, held on to it with one hand, flicking the captive now and then with another rawhide strip which was attached to a long stick.

When the captive reached the gantlet, the leash was dropped and he was given a rough shove by the chief. With his head down he tried to run forward, but his progress was slow and awkward because of the position in which his hands were tied. The Indians had worked themselves into a mad, frenzied excitement and their blows fell thick and fast. They were terrific blows. Again and again the helpless captive was knocked to the ground; but he always struggled to his feet again. He staggered; he fell; he crawled. Finally, he reached the end of the line and there he collapsed, too weak to stand.

But this was not the end of the torture. The Cherokee chief lifted the captive to his feet and stood him against a tree. He steadied his weak body while the other Indians tied him to the tree with thongs around his neck, his waist, and his ankles. Then each Indian took his turn at whipping the captive with narrow strips of rawhide and with branches cut from trees. The pain was more than the captive could endure. He shrieked aloud in his anguish. It was just what the Indians wanted. They enjoyed those loud cries of pain and anguish; those signs of weakness. They danced and leaped. They flourished their tomahawks and brandished their scalping knives.  They shouted and beat the captive more. They beat him until he scarcely breathed. Then the Indians cut the rawhide with which he was tied. Too weak to support his own weight, he fell senseless to the ground. The Cherokee chief ordered him to be turned over onto his back and bound for the final torture which would end in his death.

Jennie could not bear the sight any longer. She shut her eyes and buried her face in her hands. When at last it was all over, the shrieking of the Indians was followed by shouts of contempt and by menacing gestures in her direction.

Jennie felt that her time had come to die, that death would come to her, as it had come to her children and her brother, by the hand of a Cherokee Indian. She did not fear either pain or death. She could endure both. She would give the savages little satisfaction in torturing her if their pleasure came from shrieks of pain and cries of anguish. She would show them that she could be brave even in death. But she did want to live. She wanted to get back to her husband and her people. In a final attempt to save herself, she again appealed to the Shawnee chief for protection.

The chief turned his back to her and pretended not to hear her pleas for mercy. This was the first time he had failed to protect her from the evil intentions of the Cherokee chief. This was the first time he had failed to treat her as he would have treated his own daughter, White Fawn. His coldness gave Jennie little hope for the future.

The Indians continued to yell, to whoop, and to menace Jennie. But the Cherokee chief, for some reason, was not yet ready to torture Jennie. Perhaps he wanted to prolong the suspense. Whatever the reason, he called the Indians into a great circle around him as if he were going to address them. When their excitement had subsided and they had become quieter, he took an iron kettle from the loot the Indians had brought to the rockhouse with them. He handed it to Jennie.

"Cook meat," he commanded.

With a sense of relief at this respite from immediate torture, Jennie seized the iron kettle. She almost ran to the rockhouse. Here she filled it with bear meat and venison and swung it over a fire that was already burning. Her heart beat rapidly. For the moment, at least, her life had been spared.

On the plateau above, the Cherokee chief was holding a meeting of the council. Jennie could hear him addressing the Indians. She could hear their shouts of approval. The meeting was followed by shrieking and whooping, and by the thumping and stamping of feet in an Indian dance which continued until long after dark. Then the Cherokee chief, followed by all the Indians, came down to the rockhouse. The young captive's scalp hung from the belt of the Cherokee.

The Indians were now ready for their next victim. The Cherokee chief's attitude was no different than it had been when Jennie had earlier observed him except, perhaps, that he seemed more savage and inhuman than ever. This open hostility was shared by all the other Indians, even by the Shawnee chief. For the first time since he had claimed her as a captive, Jennie felt that he, too, was ready to do her harm.

Jennie knew the nature of the Indians. She knew that they admired bravery more than any other characteristic. Even by the members of his own tribe, only the brave Indian was permitted to survive. Could a captive expect more? Determined to show only bravery, Jennie went about her cooking as calmly as she ever went about preparing a meal for Thomas Wiley. She would keep up her courage to the end.

The Cherokee chief snatched the steaming kettle off the fire. With a deer's antler he forked some of the meat from it and placed it upon a piece of bark to cool. He paced up and down the rockhouse just as he had paced back and forth before the band of Indians only a few hours before. He stamped his feet. The other Indians acted in like manner. Finally, he grabbed the meat he had placed upon the bark to cool and with both hands full went back to the plateau above the rockhouse.

The other Indians remained in the rockhouse for a time. They ate the meat Jennie had cooked for them, they whooped, and they yelled. They made ugly gestures at Jennie with their tomahawks and scalping knives. But before long they, too, went to the plateau above the gorge, yelling, whooping, and screaming. Jennie was greatly relieved when she was alone in the rockhouse.

There was another meeting of the council. Jennie could hear the Cherokee chief talking to the Indians. She could understand little of what he said, but she knew that he was excited and angry. The torture of the captive had in no way satisfied his desire for revenge on the white settlers who had resisted him. At length his speech ended. It was followed by a repetition of the blood-curdling whoops and shouts that had preceded the torture.

Led by the Cherokee chief, a dozen Indians, all newcomers, returned to the rockhouse. The chief seized Jennie roughly by the wrists and pulled her arms as far behind her as he could. Another Indian tied her arms at the wrists and at the elbows with strips of raw deerskin.

Jennie clenched her teeth and bore the pain without uttering a sound. Believing that her time had come to die, she closed her eyes as she was led to the plateau and prayed a silent prayer that she might meet her death bravely.

Upon her arrival the dancing on the plateau ceased, and the Cherokee chief assumed command. At his direction Jennie was tied to a small white-oak tree in the same way that the young captive had been tied a few hours before. Then the Indians began to pile sticks, bark, and chunks of wood, some of which were already afire, about her.

Jennie said not a word nor moved a muscle. Somehow an inner strength came to her, wiping out all sense of fear. Her whole being seemed exalted and at peace. As she stood there in the light of the council fire, her face, her eyes, her whole proud posture reflected her calm indifference to her fate.

140

The Cherokee chief looked at her in astonishment. Such courage he had never seen, even among the members of his own race. He shouted an order. Every Indian stopped in his tracks and there was complete silence. Then the Cherokee warrior cut the thongs that bound Jennie to the stake and ordered her to return to the rockhouse.

FIVE HUNDRED SILVER BROOCHES

It was late at night when the Cherokee chief and the Shawnee chief returned to the rockhouse. They both seemed displeased, and Jennie suspected that they had quarreled.

The Cherokee chief came to Jennie and said, "White Squaw brave woman. Chief pay big price for White Squaw. Five piles silver brooches. Chief want White Squaw. Chief pay price."

Although hitherto he had always been sullen and brutal, the Cherokee's attitude and the tone of his voice now sounded less hostile than Jennie had ever heard it. Jennie looked at the Shawnee chief but he made no remark. He merely stared into the fire. He who had wanted to adopt her as his daughter was selling her for five piles of silver brooches. Why? For what purpose?

The Cherokee chief took a buckskin pouch from the pack he carried on his back and sat down on the ground before the fire with the Shawnee. He untied the drawstring of

142

the pouch and poured hundreds of silver discs about the size of a dime upon the ground. In solemn manner, he picked them up one at a time and counted them out into a pile. Then he counted out another pile, and another, and another, and another. When he was through, there were five piles of silver discs, or brooches, with a hundred in each pile.

Jennie, looking at the five piles of silver brooches, estimated that at the most they could not be worth more than five pounds in English money. "I have been sold for five pounds," she said to herself. "I am truly a slave."

The Shawnee chief opened the leather bag in which he carried his trinkets and raked the five hundred silver brooches into it contemptuously, as if he hardly cared whether he took them or not. He tossed the pouch onto the ground beside him and sat staring into the fire.

"The sale has been forced upon him," thought Jennie. "He did not want the brooches. He did not really want to sell me."

She knew that the Cherokee had always driven a hard bargain when the two chiefs had been forced to compromise. She guessed that the Shawnee had sold her in order to prevent her from being tortured. He had done it to save her life. He did, after all, think of her as he had thought of his own daughter, White Fawn.

The Cherokee chief again spoke to her. "White Squaw go with chief. Home Tennessee. White Squaw teach squaws of chief. Weave. Sew. Make dresses. Read. Write. Chief have many squaws."

An Indian could have as many squaws as he desired, provided he was rich enough to pay a dowry to the father of each squaw at the time of the wedding. Being a war chief, the Cherokee had a great number of squaws and seemed proud of the fact.

143

Jennie's heart beat rapidly. She had been saved from burning at the stake only to become the slave of a Cherokee chief whom she hated with all her heart and soul. Death itself, she thought, was more to be desired than a fate like that.

The Cherokee, now that he owned her, ordered her to lie down on her stomach and cross her wrists behind her. He tied her wrists and ankles with thongs cut from a buffalo hide, pulling the thongs so tightly that they cut into her flesh. Then, leaving her and the Shawnee chief, he joined the other Indians on the plateau.

It was Jennie's belief that he spent much of the night stretching the scalps that hung from his belt over hoops to dry. The fleshy part could then be painted red for the scalp dance, which would last for many days after his return to the Cherokee village.

At length, the day's work ended, he returned to the rock-house followed by all the other Indians. They lay down upon the ground, wheel-like around the fire, and slept as if nothing unusual had happened.

Jennie could not sleep. She had been snatched from death at the stake, yet almost wished that death had ended her misery. She was bruised in body and in mind. Not since her second night in captivity had she suffered so much. Every time she closed her eyes she saw the young man being tortured. It brought to mind the massacre of her children and her brother, and she lived through those events again. It was a night of horror.

Long before daylight the Cherokee chief was up giving orders. He untied Jennie and told her to cook meat for him. She filled the iron kettle with bear meat and venison and rekindled the fire.

"Hunt buffalo," he said to Jennie. "Then go Tennessee."

The other Indians were up. They, too, were making

144

preparations for the hunt. They all appeared happy except the Shawnee chief, who seemed greatly disturbed. He disappeared into the forest. A half hour later he returned with his arms full of leaves, roots, and barks. These he put into an earthenware vessel, which he never used for any purpose except the brewing of medicinal potions, and covered them with water. He set the mixture on the fire to simmer. When it had brewed to his satisfaction, he took it off and set it on a rock to cool.

As soon as the Indians had finished eating and were ready for the hunt, the Cherokee directed that White Squaw be tied up tightly before they left. Jennie was bound as on the night before. Though the thongs were tied so tightly that she could hardly bear it, she neither wept nor gave a sign of pain.

When the Indians started out for the hunt, the Shawnee chief lingered a while until they were out of sight. He knew that Jennie had not slept and that the shock of her recent experience had all but broken her spirit. He knew that she needed sleep. He intended that she should get it. Before he left, he carried the earthenware vessel containing the sleeping potion to Jennie. He lifted her head gently with his left hand and with his right he held the vessel to her lips. "White Squaw drink," he said. "White Squaw sleep."

Jennie drank the sleeping potion. Then the chief disappeared into the forest.

JENNIE'S DREAM

The sleeping potion had the effect the Shawnee chief desired. Soon after drinking it, Jennie's aches and pains left her. Her muscles relaxed. Her heartbeat became slower, and her breathing was easier. She dropped into a deep sleep.

She dreamed — or seemed to dream, for the dream was more like a vision than a dream — that she was on the plateau where the young man had been tortured. She saw him bound for torture. Then the strips of rawhide with which he had been tied vanished, and he arose and stood beside her.

"Oh! Oh!" she shrieked in pity, as she looked upon his bloody, tortured figure.

The young man put his finger on his lips as a sign for her to keep silent. In his left hand, he carried the skull of a sheep that was partially filled with buffalo tallow. A short wick set into the tallow burned with a tiny flickering flame. The young man said not a word, but beckoned Jennie to follow him.

146

Jennie's own bonds fell away from her and she felt herself moving strangely through space without any effort of her own. She was following the brightly burning flame of the light carried by the young man. They moved down the gorge, across the narrow bottom through which ran Little Mudlick Creek. They followed the creek to Big Mudlick and thence to Big Paint Creek. They crossed Big Paint Creek and went into the hills on the other side. They crossed creeks, climbed hills, and walked along ridges. They seemed to move as lightly and as gently as a breeze. At last they came to the top of a high hill overlooking a big river.

The young man blew upon his small fluttering lamp and the tiny flame suddenly became a great glowing light which revealed the entire valley as clearly as if it were midday.

On the far side of the river was a fort and near it moved white women and children. Jennie could hear the voices of the children as they called to each other in a game of wood tag. She wanted to call out to them, but while she was looking at them, the light from the candle slowly dimmed to a fluttering flame again. It flickered in the wind for a moment, and then went out.

Jennie tried to rub her eyes, but her hands were tied behind her. Her ankles were tied. She lay upon the ground, just as the Indians had left her.

"Was it a dream?" she asked herself. "Was it a dream? It all seemed so real. There were white women and children. The children were playing wood tag. It couldn't be a dream. But yes it was — it must have been — a dream."

She rolled over on her left side and went to sleep again. The dream was repeated. This time the dream seemed even more real than it had the first time, but upon arousing from her slumber, she found herself bound hand and foot, as before. She was more bewildered than ever.

147

"I don't understand," she said to herself. "It was all so real. There was a fort. There were women and children. There were white people. My people!"

While she was trying to remember the dream, she went to sleep again, and the dream was repeated a third time. Again Jennie awoke to find herself still bound hand and foot. However, she felt rested. The sleeping potion had brought her relaxation and a feeling of tranquillity. She was thinking clearly. "Was it a dream?" she wondered. "Was it just a dream? It was all so real. I saw the fort. I saw the women and children and heard them!"

She continued to talk to herself. "The young man — he who had been tortured to death on the plateau — led me. We went down the gorge, across the bottom. We crossed Big Paint Creek. We crossed other creeks. We climbed hills. But in which direction? I can't remember."

A terrific storm was raging. Great sheets of rain were coming up the narrow gorge outside the rockhouse. There was thunder and lightning. The trees were swaying. It was the kind of storm she had witnessed the night the Indians had forced her to swim Tug River.

"Tug River," thought Jennie. "It was at Tug River that the Indians eluded Tice Harman. They escaped in a blinding rain. I can do likewise. This is my chance. I shall take advantage of it."

Jennie kept on talking to herself. "The Cherokee chief will hunt buffalo today and tomorrow. Upon his return the next day, he will start to the Cherokee villages in Tennessee. If he succeeds in taking me there, I shall become a slave to his tribe of Indians. This dream is a sign that now is the time to make my escape."

Jennie knew that when she tried to escape she would be followed by the Indians. Her only chance of success lay in putting as much distance as possible between herself and

148

them before they returned to the rockhouse, and in making her trail as hard to follow as she could.

"If I am caught," she thought, "death will follow. But death is better than a life of slavery among the Cherokee Indians. I will make an effort to escape."

Rain was blowing into the lower corner of the rockhouse. "If I roll over there and lie in the rain," she thought, "the rawhide thongs will become wet. They will stretch and perhaps I can slip my hands out of them."

She was thankful that the Indians had not lashed her to the rock as they sometimes did when they went away and left her alone in the rockhouse.

She rolled over and over until she reached the spot where the rain fell upon her. It was a cold, drenching rain. It came down on her head and shoulders. It ran down her neck. Only her garments of heavy leather prevented her from becoming completely soaked to the skin.

She lay upon her stomach so that the rain could beat upon her wrists, which were tied behind her. She tried to move her wrists, but at first, swollen as they were, it was difficult and painful. She tried again and again and again. At last the thongs gave a little and she could move one wrist upon the other. The slight loosening of the thongs encouraged her, and she renewed her efforts.

Finally she had stretched the wet rawhide strips until she was able to slip her hands through them. It was an easy matter then to untie the thongs that bound her ankles. At last she was in a position to make her dash for freedom.

It was gray and misty outside the rockhouse. Rain was still falling. It was difficult to tell the time of day, but Jennie guessed it was about midmorning.

The Indians had left before daylight. "Even if they have taken shelter under overhanging rocks during the storm," she thought, "they must be well on their way to the buffalo lick. I shall flee in the opposite direction so that there will not be any danger of meeting them."

She called her dog. "Here, Tige," she said. "I must leave you here."

Poor Tige! He had been her companion for eleven months. She had talked to him at times as if he were a person and he had seemed to listen. How she hated to leave him with the Indians!

But this was no time for sentiment. If she were going to try to make an escape, she must not risk the barking of

a dog. She must not risk the trail he might leave. She must not take him with her. She could take no chances.

She made a muzzle of leather and slipped it over his nose and head. This was to keep him from barking when she left. Then she tied him to the stone to which she, herself, had been tied so many times. She patted him on the head. "There, now, Tige," she said. "There now. Sometime, perhaps —"

Jennie did not finish her sentence. She knew that she had no time to lose. She must think about the present, not about the future.

"What do I need to carry with me?" she asked herself. "Just as little as possible."

She took enough meat to supply her with food for a day or two. "After that," she thought, "if I am fortunate enough to get away, I shall find food in the same way the Indians find it — by hunting for it."

She might need to fight for her life. "What is there I can use for a weapon?" she wondered.

By searching the possessions of the Indians which had been left in the rockhouse, she found a warrior's belt holding a scalping knife and a tomahawk. She tied the belt around her waist. "This is all I shall take," she decided.

On leaving the rockhouse Jennie followed the path, which was full of running water, up the gorge to a place where she could step into Little Mudlick Creek without leaving footprints. She waded down Little Mudlick Creek to the place where it empties into Big Mudlick Creek. She waded Big Mudlick Creek to its junction with Big Paint Creek.

Big Paint Creek was overflowing its banks. The current was swift and the water was deep. Without a minute's hesitation, Jennie dived into the muddy water and tried to swim to the opposite side. In the middle of the stream she was caught in a swirling pool and was almost drowned before she could pull herself up onto a floating treetop. She rode the floating treetop to the mouth of the stream that now bears her name, Jennie's Creek, where she slipped into the quiet backwater. She swam up Jennie's Creek until she

151

found the water shallow enough for wading. Then she waded the creek to its forks.

Here she was confused. She did not know which fork to take. She recalled the dream and went over it in her mind, but the dream told her nothing. After the young man had taken her across Big Paint Creek, they had gone forward, in what direction she did not know. She remembered only that in her dream she had seen a big river and a fort on the other side of it. That part of her dream had been completely real. How far away had it been? In which direction? She could not tell.

In marching with the Indians she had noticed that when they were in unfamiliar territory they gave little thought to the direction of their march. They had followed a general sense of direction and they had always come out at the place where they wanted to be. She, too, would follow instinct. Since her first impulse had been to take the left fork, this fork she took, believing it would lead her to the big river she had seen in her dream.

She waded the left fork, Lick Fork of Jennie's Creek, to the Middle Fork, where, again, she instinctively turned to the left. She waded this stream for a distance and then waded one of its branches to its source. She crossed a divide through a low gap and descended another stream known as Bear Branch, to Little Paint Creek. She continued down this stream to its mouth where she found water that was too deep for wading.

For almost twenty hours, by day and by night, she had waded swollen streams. The night had been stormy. Only twice had she stopped, and then just long enough to eat a few bites of meat. She sat down by the edge of the water to gather strength, to give thanks for her safety, so far, and to wait for daylight so that she could see where she was before proceeding further.

152

Jennie knew the Indians would follow her just as soon as they returned to the rockhouse and found her gone. "At best," she thought, "I could not have been gone more than eight hours before they made this discovery."

Much of the time she had traveled very slowly, especially during the time when she had had to cling to the treetop that carried her around the bend in Big Paint Creek.

The Indians, once they had picked up her trail, would travel much faster than she had traveled. They would not need to wade streams to cover their tracks as she had done. They would take short cuts, too. Her greatest hope for time to complete her escape lay in the thought that she had not left a trail that could be picked up easily.

Except that she was, apparently, beside a larger and deeper river than any she had met so far, Jennie did not know what was before her. She must simply wait until daylight and the lifting of the fog to survey her surroundings.

MOMENTS OF SUSPENSE

As the first gray streaks of dawn showed in the eastern sky, Jennie could see the dim outline of a high bank overlooking a river. "God be praised," she said. "This must be the river I saw in my dream."

The morning was dull and cloudy, and a foggy mist almost hid the river. Until the fog lifted and she could see to the farther side of the river there was nothing Jennie could do but sit and wait. She looked about her with mixed feelings. She was happy, yet she was frightened.

"What if there is no fort on the other side of the river?" she asked herself. "What if the Indians come before I can cross the river?" These and other questions raced through her mind.

In the forest behind her, a squirrel jumped from one limb to another. It did not make a great noise, but it was enough to startle Jennie and make her spring to her feet. Her nerves were on edge. "There now," she said to herself, "I must not let a squirrel frighten me. I must keep calm."

She sat down again and waited for day to break. When morning came, the fog would surely lift. How slowly the time passed. At first she could see only the water, then willow trees, then the bank on the farther side, then, at last, a clearing. "Oh!" she shouted, "Oh! Oh! This is the river of my dream! This is the river!" Over and over she repeated, happily, "This is the river! This is the river!"

154

The fog drifted from the valley into the chain of broken hills back of it. The sun was beginning to break through in places. Jennie shaded her eyes with her hand and peered into the clearing. "There is the fort," she said. "It is real. I am not dreaming. There is the fort."

The fort was Harman's Station. It was the fort that Tice and the men from Walker's Gap had been planning to build in the autumn of Jennie's capture. And after that short hunt which had ended so disastrously, they *had* built it. Here it was! It stood not more than three hundred feet from the bank of the river. All the trees and undergrowth from the fort to the riverbank had been cut, and an equal distance around the fort on each of the other three sides had been cleared. With this clearing it was impossible for Indians to attack the fort without being seen before they could reach it.

The fort itself was about twenty feet square and two stories high. The walls of both stories had loopholes through which to fire in case the Indians attacked. The door of the fort, made of heavy oak timbers six inches thick, was hung on great wooden hinges. It opened inward and could be securely barred by a huge oak beam. With the beam in place, it was almost impossible to open the door from the outside. On all four sides the upper story was built two feet wider than the lower story. This extra space was floored with heavy oak timbers in which loopholes were cut. If Indians should ever manage to get into the fort, the defenders could take refuge on the second floor and through these loopholes they could fire upon the Indians from above.

As Jennie stood gazing upon the fort, she saw some women walking toward it. They were carrying buckets of water from a small stream which flowed close by the fort. Children played about them, chasing each other from one piece of wood to another.

"Wood tag," said Jennie. "That is what they were playing in my dream."

She called to the women, but they kept on walking toward the fort. The lapping of the water on the banks of the river and the rustling of a light wind in the trees kept her cries from reaching their ears. In desperation she screamed, "Save me! Oh, save me! Save me from the Indians."

The sound of her cries was heard but not the words, and the sound seemed to frighten the women and children. They hurried into the fort and closed the gate behind them.

Jennie wrung her hands and screamed again and again. "The Indians! The Indians! Save me from the Indians!"

At last an old man came out of the fort and walked toward the river.

Jennie called to him, "Save me! Please save me! Save me from the Indians!"

"Who are you?" the old man asked.

"Jennie Wiley," she shouted at the top of her voice.

"Jennie?" the old man cried. "Jennie Wiley! Praise be! Of course, we will save you."

"Henry Skaggs! Henry Skaggs!" shouted Jennie. "Oh! Oh! Oh! Henry Skaggs!"

How fast Jennie's heart seemed to beat within her! Here was someone who knew her. Here at last was a friend!

She told Henry Skaggs how she had escaped from the Cherokee chief less than twenty-four hours before. "He will be following me. He'll be here any minute," she cried. "Help me! Oh, help me!"

Henry Skaggs knew the Cherokee chief and understood Jennie's fears. "We'll save you, Jennie," he said. "We'll get you across the river before the Cherokee gets here. The men have gone from the fort with the canoes," he went on, "and I shall have to make a raft before I can cross the river, but I'll save you. Keep up your courage! If the Indians should come in sight before I can get there, start swimming. We'll get you across one way or another."

Many of the women had come down to the riverbank by this time. They, too, knew Jennie Wiley. For eleven months they had talked about her, wondered about her fate, hoped for her rescue.

"Get the axes," Henry Skaggs said to them.

On the bank of the river stood a tree that had been struck by lightning years before. Part of its main growth had been ripped off at the time. Since then the bark and many of the smaller limbs had dried and dropped off. What was left of it stood straight and tall. Henry Skaggs and two of the women took turns chopping the tree down, and the chips fell fast. Other women cut long, slender grapevines, pulled them out of the tops of tall trees, and carried them to the water's edge.

When the tree fell, it broke into several pieces of about the same length. These pieces were rolled into the river and tied together with the grapevines. Wherever the ends of the vines met and wherever the vines crossed, they were

158

tied with strips of leather. Within a short time a small raft was ready.

Henry Skaggs tied strips of leather to two long rifles. These he slung across his back and shoulders with muzzles pointed downward to keep the powder free from any splashing water. Then taking a long pole from the wood-yard for shoving, and a shorter one for paddling, he pushed out into the swift, muddy current.

As a matter of safety all of the children and some of the women were sent back to the fort. A few women stayed upon the bank of the river to help with the landing when Henry returned with Jennie.

The raft drifted with the current and Henry Skaggs did not try to prevent it. All of his efforts were directed toward getting it to the other side of the river. He made rapid progress considering the swiftness of the current he had to cross, but to Jennie, fearful that the Indians might appear at any minute, his progress seemed terribly slow.

Now that she had discovered there were white people so close to Little Mudlick Falls, she believed that the Indians had known it all the time. She had never been taken with them when they had hunted in this direction. She remembered, too, that most of the scouting parties which had visited them had come from this direction. She was sure that the Indians, believing she knew that white people were at the fort, would suspect that she had fled to this very spot. If so, it could not be long before they would arrive. She ran along the riverbank wringing her hands, hoping and praying, and keeping even with the raft as it floated down the river.

The women on the east bank of the river walked downstream with the raft, too. They, also, expected that the Indians would appear at any moment, as did Henry Skaggs. Everyone's heart was filled with anxiety.

The moment the raft touched the bank Jennie jumped upon it. She threw her arms around the old man and clung to him for a moment. Then she seized the paddle, and they both put forth every effort to get the raft back to the east bank of the river.

The current in midstream was swift, and the raft was hard to manage. In spite of all they could do, it caught in a treetop which had already picked up a mass of driftwood and debris. The raft was almost pulled to pieces, but the grapevines held. The tough pieces of leather did not break.

By skillful use of the long pole and the short paddle, Henry Skaggs and Jennie, once out of the current, steered the whole drift in which the raft had been caught to the east bank of the river. It was hard work, but at last they were close enough to the bank for the women to throw them one end of a long grapevine. Jennie tied the grapevine to the raft. The women pulled, Henry Skaggs pushed with the long pole, and Jennie paddled with the short one. In this manner the raft, with all the drift it had collected, was brought beneath some overhanging willows. Henry and

Jennie seized the branches and pulled the raft to the bank of the river. Then, holding to another long grapevine, one end of which the women had drawn tightly around the trunk of a tree, they climbed to the top of the bank.

Jennie dropped down upon the ground and kissed it. The women dropped down beside her with loving words of joy and encouragement. Henry Skaggs stood and looked on while tears of happiness dimmed his eyes.

On the west side of the river, there was a sudden commotion. Henry Skaggs, Jennie, and the other women looked in that direction. There stood the Cherokee chief, accompanied by more than twenty stalwart Indians. Jennie's dog was with them. He sniffed at her tracks upon the bank, looked across the river, and barked.

"White Squaw, come back! Come back!" the Cherokee shouted.

Jennie, for the first time since she had been taken captive, defied him.

"Honor, White Squaw! Honor!" he shouted. "War Chief saved White Squaw's life! War Chief not let White Squaw burn. War Chief buy White Squaw with silver brooches."

Henry Skaggs lifted a long rifle. He took deliberate aim at the Cherokee chief. He fired, but the distance was too great. The bullet fell into the water.

The Cherokee chief shot an arrow in return but it, too, fell into the water. Then he gave a war whoop and he and his Indians disappeared in the forest.

Jennie's dog, unnoticed by the Indians, stayed behind. He ran back and forth along the water's edge, sniffing at Jennie's footsteps there, whimpering a little, and occasionally stopping to look across the river.

When the Indians were out of sight and sound, Jennie knelt by the water's edge. She held out her hands and called, "Tige! Tige! Come, Tige!"

161

With a bark of joy, Tige leaped into the river and holding his head well above water, set out paddling for the other shore. When he reached midstream, the current took him, but he still paddled bravely forward. Jennie walked along the bank, calling to him, and encouraging him as his progress toward her was slowed by the swift water. Once, as a drifting branch caught him, his head almost went under but he freed himself and kept on. Jennie called, "Good dog, Tige. Come on, Tige."

Finally he was out of the current. Finally he was almost within reach of Jennie's outstretched hand. Finally his feet touched bottom.

"Tige, Tige," said Jennie. "You made it, Tige. You made it. We're both free!"

For a minute Tige, panting, was almost too tired to bark. Then he shook himself, and with wildly wagging tail and happy little yelps, jumped on Jennie. For another minute they stood there at the edge of the water, Jennie patting him and saying words of praise and welcome. Then, together, they clambered up the bank and walked toward the fort.

Relieved from the terrible strain she had been under, Jennie found herself suddenly weak and dreadfully tired. Her one thought, now that she was free, was to get home; to get back to her husband. But she found that she must wait a day or two to gather strength for this last part of her long, long journey.

How was Thomas? she asked her friends. Was he in despair? Had he thought, after so long a time, that she would never escape? Had he given her up as lost forever?

No, they told her. When he had heard Tice Harman's report of her capture he was thankful that she was still alive. He had said, "She will escape. She will come back to me."

He had rebuilt the cabin, they said, repaired the furniture, and put things in order as they had been on the afternoon when Jennie had been taken captive. Day in and day out he had lived there alone, waiting for her return.

"Oh, Thomas!" cried Jennie, as she listened. "I will be there soon."

A few days after that Thomas was seated at the table in his cabin eating his lonely supper when there was a bark outside and, a moment later, a familiar knock at the door — two quick knocks, and then another. He was startled! It was the knock that he and Jennie had used as a signal!

He listened. The knock was repeated.

Thomas Wiley arose from the split-log bench and walked to the door. His knees trembled. His hands shook. Could it be Jennie?

He took down the crossbar, turned the buttons that held the door shut, and opened the door.

"Jennie!" he cried. "Oh, Jennie!"

Jennie fell into his arms. She was home at last!

Published with the
assistance of the staff at

Jenny Wiley State Resort Park

75 Theatre Court
Prestonsburg, KY 41653-9799
(606) 886-2711